Italian Cooking

Anne Ager

Contents

First published in 1982 by Octopus Books Limited
59 Grosvenor Street, London W1

Second impression,1982

© 1982 Hennerwood Publications Limited

ISBN 0 86273 025 2

Printed in England by Severn Valley Press Limited

INTRODUCTION

Italian cooking can quite genuinely be regarded as one of the true 'mother cuisines', and as a symbol of Latin culture today. The ancient Romans created the original Italian cuisine, gleaning much inspiration from Asia Minor and Greece. Making the most of home-grown produce and their acquired culinary knowledge, the Romans were able to pass on to many other cultures, including the French, the real meaning of good cooking and stylish eating.

If you want to know why the Italians eat the way they do, look back to the Renaissance. It is Catherine di Medici who was really responsible for the spread of Italian culinary knowledge. She travelled to France in the early sixteenth century, for her marriage to Henry II, accompanied by teams of master cooks. These 'aristocrats of the kitchen' passed on their secrets to the willing and eager French – secrets of the most sophisticated cooking that had yet been developed. The Medici cooks impressed their recipients with a variety of featherlight sweets and pastries, and many dishes containing what were, at that time, rare and unusual vegetables – such as artichokes, broccoli and baby peas (now adopted by the French as 'petits pois'). Amongst their favoured ingredients, the Medici cooks imported truffles, and they encouraged the French to start digging for their own.

Renaissance Italy was famed for its excessively sweet tooth, and many of the luscious Italian desserts stem from this period. Cane sugar from Venice was used by the rich in almost any food, including pasta. This habit was far too expensive for the poorer people, and they had to eat their pasta unsweetened, as we choose to do now.

To some people, the cooking of Italy means pasta, and more pasta – a world of spaghetti, macaroni and noodles, too monotonous to comprise anything more exciting and titillating to the palate. What a terrible misconception. The Italian repertory of food is one of the most colourful, flavourful and exhilarating; ranging from rich, hearty soups, multitudinous varieties of antipasti, and delicately herbed meat and fish, to a bountiful selection of cheeses, mouth-watering desserts and ice creams.

Styles of cooking vary very much from one part of Italy to another, because the Italians make use of local and seasonal products. The most noticeable culinary division is that between north and south. The cooking of the north reflects the more prosperous elements of that part of the country, where butter is the most common cooking fat, meat is produced and eaten in great abundance, and ribbon-shaped noodles are made from an egg-enriched dough. In the poorer south, cheaper ingredients are used; olive oil in place of butter (it costs less to support an olive tree than a cow, and the tree can survive on poor soil), and manufactured tubular pasta, such as spaghetti. Less meat is eaten in the south of the country, and the most important sources of protein are locally caught fish and homemade cheese.

All great cuisines are based fundamentally on the cooking of the peasants. Italy's cooking has remained relatively uncorrupted due to the fact that the four most important staple foods of the country still go into the knapsack of every field worker, woodsman and fisherman – bread, cheese, sausage, and, more often than not, wine. These foods are so much a part of the Italian diet, that some are now known by the name of the place that produced them, e.g., Gorgonzola cheese, Orvieto wine, and boloney sausage from Bologna.

Bread is without doubt one of the important foods to the average Italian, and, if he is lucky enough to live outside the cities he can still enjoy real homemade bread, shaped into simple round loaves. Bread is rarely spread with butter in Italy, and almost never toasted. Broken pieces of dry bread are eaten at most stages of a meal, often with pasta, and even sometimes dunked into a glass of red wine.

After pasta, which one has to regard as being one of the other staple specialities, produce from the sea is the next most important category of food in Italy. Every Italian province bordering on to the sea has its own speciality fish dishes, and there are few provinces that do not border on to the coast at some point.

The Italian fishermen catch in excess of 700 million pounds of fish each year, including red mullet, anchovies, sardines, tunny, oysters, clams, spiny lobsters and crayfish, to name just a few.

The quality of fruit and vegetables in Italy is extremely high – the tomatoes are plump, rich and fruity; the lemons seem to look more yellow, and the peppers are smooth and shiny. Many theories have been put forward to explain this. It could be the sea mists, rich in mineral salts; the predominant use of natural rather than artificial fertilizers; or just the loving hand of the Italian fruit and vegetable grower.

Part of Italy's brilliance in cooking lies in the careful, subtle and yet frequent use of herbs. The variety is extensive, and few Italian kitchens are to be seen without a bunch or two of basil, marjoram, thyme, rosemary, oregano and myrtle. Spices such as coriander, saffron and ginger lend their own distinctive flavours to many Italian specialities, and garlic is an indispensible part of the Italian kitchen.

Rice is almost as important to the Italians as is pasta, and is a highly prized item in Italian agriculture. Italy is the largest producer of rice in Europe. The Italians cook their rice as they do their pasta, 'al dente', and are greatly critical of other countries who overcook it to a solid 'pudding'.

The quality of meat reared in Italy is particularly good, especially veal which is the most popular variety. And what of the sausage? Every region, every city, every town seems to have its own special type of sausage – some sharply spiced with garlic, some studded with peppercorns, and some tingling with ginger. And there are the cured pork products of Italy, the hams. Parma and San Daniele are the two varieties prized by the connoisseurs, and both can be found on sale in this country.

Poultry and game are extremely popular in certain regions of the country, and ducks, pheasants, quail and hare all find their way on to the Italian table.

When it comes to Italian cheeses, the list is almost endless. Apart from the many varieties to be found on sale in shops and on market stalls, there are also the formaggi casalinga – the so-called peasant cheese, made on a small scale at home, for consumption by family and friends. The most well known cheeses of the Italian mainland are Parmesan, Pecorino, Ricotta, Bel Paese and Gorgonzola (more about these and other cheeses on the right and page 6).

The quantity of cakes eaten by Italians is prodigious, and such is their sweet tooth that they even eat sweet biscuits or macaroons with their lunchtime aperitifs. Spices play a large part in Italian confectionery, as do candied fruits, nuts, and Ricotta cheese. The sweet dishes served at home in Italy are on the whole very simple; the towering confections of sponge, cream and nuts are very much the prerogative of the restaurants and smart bars.

THE ITALIAN STORE CUPBOARD

Most of the ingredients listed here are integral parts of Italian cooking, essential to the authentic flavour of a particular dish. It is not always possible to find some of these ingredients in England, and, where this is the case, alternatives are suggested.

OLIVE OIL There really is no substitute for olive oil, and the use of cooking oil in its place will spoil the chosen recipe. Although olive oil is relatively expensive, there are several different quality grades, and you can always choose one of the cheaper ones. Like most bulk purchases, it works out cheaper if you buy a large quantity at a time. Do not store olive oil at too cold a temperature, otherwise it starts to go cloudy. If this happens, warm it gently. Olive oil is used in very generous quantities by the Italians. If you do not like an excessively oily flavour, reduce the given quantities slightly.

CHEESES Although not all these cheeses are available in Great Britain, it is interesting to be aware of the variety, particularly if you have the chance to travel to Italy itself.
Asiago: a fairly hard cheese made from skimmed and unskimmed cows' milk. It has a granular, pasty texture, peppered with tiny holes, and the flavour is slightly sharp. Use as a table cheese, or for grating. (Venezia, Friuli and Lombardy)
Bel Paese: a soft creamy cheese, with a somewhat bland flavour. It melts easily and is a perfect cooking cheese. (Lombardy)
Bitto: a hard, fat cheese made from cows' and ewes' milk, perforated with holes like Emmenthal. It can be eaten 'young', while it is still soft and mild, or left to mature for a year or two. The flavour becomes sharper, and the texture firmer, so that it is suitable for grating. (Lombardy)

Butirri: a variety of Caciocavallo. The cheese is shaped like an elongated fir cone, with a piece of butter embedded in the centre of the cheese. (Calabria and Campania)

Caciocavallo: a spindle-shaped cheese, most usually made from cows' milk. The small cheeses are strung together in pairs and hung over a pole to mature, like a saddle (hence the name, the translation of which is 'cheese on horseback'). When fresh, the cheese is soft and smooth; when fully matured it is firm enough to grate. (Sicily and Naples)

Caciotta: a mild cheese with a fairly indistinct flavour. In Tuscany it is made from ewes' milk; in Umbria from cows' milk; and in Capri from goats' milk.

Canestrato: a yellow cheese made from ewes' milk, with a strong salty flavour. This is one of the most popular Sicilian cheeses – it is moulded into baskets, and left until it is hard enough to grate.

Caso Forte: this is a strong, sharp-flavoured cheese, which is served at the beginning of a meal to act as an appetite stimulant. (Naples)

Castelmagno: similar to Gorgonzola, this is one of the many Italian 'blue' cheeses. It is a sharp salty cheese with a strong herb flavour. (Piedmont)

Casu Marzu: one of the 'oddity' cheeses – its soft texture has a very pungent flavour, highly thought of by many cheese connoisseurs. (Sardinia)

Crescenza: a delicate-flavoured cheese, combining the flavours of cheese, butter and cream. (Milan)

Dolcelatte: a mild and creamy 'blue' cheese. In prime condition this is one of Italy's best cheeses.

Fior d'Alpe: a soft, creamy cheese with an elastic texture and herby flavour. This cheese is made from cows' milk all year round. (Milan)

Fior di Latte: this is an unsalted cheese, and the name means 'flower of the milk'. If the cheese is eaten when very fresh, it is said to squeak in the mouth. Similar to Mozzarella.

Fiore Molle: a soft, creamy coloured cheese with a slightly salty flavour. Saffron is sometimes added to the cheese during making. (Lazio)

Fontina: a truly wonderful cheese. It has a brown crust rather like Gruyère, and comes in large wheels. The texture is fairly firm, cream white in colour, and peppered with tiny holes. It has a nutty sweet flavour with a distinct tang, and is a perfect melting cheese. If you find it difficult to obtain, use Bel Paese instead. (Piedmont)

Formaggio Fiore: a hard textured white cheese, with a sharp flavour – rather similar to Pecorino. Used mainly as a grating cheese. (Sardinia)

Gorgonzola: a very good blue cheese, which is matured in damp caves to develop the characteristic mould. It has a unique creamy soft texture, with a sharp flavour. There is also a slightly bitter-flavoured, white Gorgonzola. (Gorgonzola and Milan)

Grana Lodi: a fine-grained, hard, yellow cheese, similar to Parmesan, but stronger and sharper in flavour. It is often pitted with holes. (Lombardy)

Mascherpone: just like clotted cream, it is buttery in colour and rich in flavour. Sometimes mixed with rum and sugar and served as a sweet. (Lombardy)

Mozzarella: a soft snow-white cheese, with a smooth slightly rubbery texture. The best mozzarellas are made from buffaloes' milk, and the cheeses are left, paper-wrapped, immersed in their own whey to keep them fresh. It is an excellent cooking cheese. (Campania and Naples)

Pagliarini: a cows' milk cheese, with a slightly sharp flavour, which is sold on a straw base. (Piedmont)

Pannerone: a creamy cheese, with a distinct sharp flavour – similar to Gorgonzola but without the mould.

Parmesan: one of the best cheeses in the world. A golden-yellow, solid compact cheese, with a characteristic sharp flavour and a 'grainy' texture. Parmesan is *the* grating cheese – it comes in several different grades and is excellent for cooking. (Reggio-Emilia)

Pecorino: this is a firm cheese, usually yellow in colour – the texture is hard and dry, yet smooth. The colour of the rind varies very much from one region to another. When very young, Pecorino can be used as a table cheese; when fully mature it is used as a grating cheese. If you find it difficult to obtain, use Parmesan instead. (Lazio, Umbria, Lucca and Sardinia)

Provatura: a soft white cheese, made from buffaloes' milk. It is shaped like a large egg and must be eaten very fresh. (Rome)

Provola: a soft cheese made from buffaloes' milk – it is sometimes lightly smoked to give a mature flavour. (Campania)

Provolone: similar to Provola, but more common – it is now made from cows' milk. It comes in various amusing shapes such as pigs, pears and little men. The cheeses are wrapped in string which gives the rind its characteristic marking. The young cheese is delicate and creamy, but it becomes sharper and spicier as it gets older. (Campania)

Ricotta: this white curd cheese is made throughout Italy and is used widely in cooking, both sweet and savoury dishes. It is a soft unsalted cheese, with a distinct flavour. If you find it difficult to obtain, use drained and sieved cottage cheese.

Robiola: a very soft cheese, rich and fairly strong in flavour. It is pressed and shaped into squares or rounds. The flavour of the mature cheese is said to resemble that of truffles. (N. Italy)

Robiolini: a soft, smooth cheese with a distinctive flavour – firmer than Robiola. (Piedmont and Lombardy)

Scamorza: similar to Mozzarella, it is soft and mild, and a good cooking cheese. (Abruzzi)

Stracchino: a smooth, creamy coloured cheese with a mild flavour.

Teleggio: a fat, pale yellow soft cheese, with a thin pink rind – it is similar to Stracchino with an aromatic flavour.

Tomino: a rather special goats' milk cheese, which is preserved in pepper. (Piedmont)

SAUSAGES, HAMS AND OTHER CURED MEATS The wide variety of Italian slicing sausages and cured meat products is endless. Quite a good selection of the products is available in this country, and it is well worth looking out for the following – Salame di Milano, a medium coarse salami, well seasoned, but not too strong in flavour; Bressaola, a mountain cured beef, which is cut into very thin slices; Parma ham, which is an air cured pork product, and one of the most popular Italian 'cold meats' – served in paper thin slices; and San Daniele, which is very similar to Parma ham, but it has a slightly superior flavour, is more expensive and not so readily available. If a recipe calls for Parma ham or San Daniele and you find them difficult to buy, use a good quality smoked ham instead. There are also, of course, the small whole Italian sausages, much coarser in texture than the English varieties and quite spicy – some are suitable for grilling, while others are intended to be boiled.

RICE Is a major ingredient in many Italian dishes, and it is important to use the correct type of rice, especially with a risotto – look out for the round-grained Italian Arborio rice. If a recipe specifies long grain rice, it is preferable to use an Italian variety but not essential.

PASTA Not everyone is going to attempt to make their own pasta – even the average Italian housewife keeps a stock of dry spaghetti, vermicelli, and pasta shapes. They are excellent store cupboard standbys as a base for a quick meal. Make sure that they are kept in a dry cupboard, in a sealed packet.

HERBS Fresh herbs give a better flavour to a dish than the dried ones, but it is not always possible to buy them and only a small percentage of people actually grow them. If you wish to grow a selection of herbs at home, then the following types are those most frequently used in Italian cooking: sweet basil, sage, thyme, marjoram, tarragon. Parsley is used in great profusion and oregano is also used in certain dishes.

If you are using dried herbs in place of fresh ones, then use 1×5 ml spoon/1 teaspoon of the dried herb in place of every 1×15 ml/1 tablespoon of chopped fresh herb.

DRIED MUSHROOMS Used in small quantities they make a good addition to soups and sauces. They must be soaked in warm water for 15–20 minutes, prior to using. They are quite expensive to buy, but as they are used in relatively small quantities, one packet goes quite a long way.

TRUFFLES Truffles are used frequently in high class Italian cooking, but not by the average Italian housewife – both the black and white truffles are very expensive to buy. If you wish to add that 'rather special flavour' to a dish you can use truffle paste – it comes in a tube and is available at a reasonable price from most speciality food shops.

SOUPS

You may well be slightly confused on being offered soup in Italy, and wonder whether you are actually eating your pasta course. The Italians frequently add pasta to their soups, sometimes in a small quantity, and sometimes with such generosity that your spoon will almost stand up in it! This does not mean that all Italian soups contain pasta, far from it, as some are based solely on vegetables. The Italian housewife prides herself on making a good flavourful homemade soup, more often than not based on proper stock. For those who have the time, there are recipes in this section for chicken and beef stock; and, for those who do not, use a good quality stock cube.

Brodo di pollo
Chicken stock

Metric	Imperial
1 large boiling chicken, giblets removed	1 large boiling chicken, giblets removed
1 veal bone (about 225 g)	1 veal bone (about 8 oz)
3.5 litres water	6 pints water
3 carrots, scraped	3 carrots, scraped
1 large onion, peeled and stuck with 3 cloves	1 large onion, peeled and stuck with 3 cloves
2 sticks celery, roughly chopped	2 sticks celery, roughly chopped
2 leeks, washed and roughly chopped	2 leeks, washed and roughly chopped
1 × 5 ml spoon crushed peppercorns	1 teaspoon crushed peppercorns
1 × 5 ml spoon blade mace	1 teaspoon blade mace
handful of parsley stalks	handful of parsley stalks
1 × 2.5 ml spoon salt	½ teaspoon salt

Preparation time: 5 minutes
Cooking time: 3¼ hours

For a soup this stock can be cleared in the same way as for Brodo di Manzo. Remove any fat that forms if you store the stock in the refrigerator.

Put the chicken into a large pan with the veal bone and water. Bring slowly to the boil, removing all the scum that rises to the surface.
Add the remaining ingredients. Bring back to the boil, cover and simmer for 3 hours. Strain through muslin or a fine sieve before using.
The cooked chicken can be made into a risotto, or Pollo in Salsa Tonnato (page 62).
Makes 1.75 litres/3 pints

Brodo di manzo
Beef stock

Metric
1 kg beef bones, with a
  small amount of meat on
3 carrots, scraped
2 medium onions, peeled
3.5 litres water
450 g stewing beef
2 leeks, washed and
  roughly chopped
2 sticks celery, roughly
  chopped
handful of parsley stalks
1 × 5 ml spoon crushed
  peppercorns
1 × 2.5 ml spoon salt
3 × 15 ml spoons tomato
  purée

Imperial
2 lb beef bones, with a
  small amount of meat on
3 carrots, scraped
2 medium onions, peeled
6 pints water
1 lb stewing beef
2 leeks, washed and
  roughly chopped
2 sticks celery, roughly
  chopped
handful of parsley stalks
1 teaspoon crushed
  peppercorns
½ teaspoon salt
3 tablespoons tomato
  purée

Preparation time: 10 minutes
Cooking time: 3¾ hours
Oven: 200°, 400°F, Gas Mark 6

This stock keeps well in the refrigerator for 4–5 days. All the fat which forms on the surface must be skimmed off before using. If you wish to serve the stock as a clear soup, put the strained stock into a saucepan with 2 crushed egg shells and 2 stiffly beaten egg whites. Bring to the boil, stirring continuously, and strain through muslin or a fine sieve.

Put the beef bones, carrots and onions into a roasting tin. Place in a preheated oven and cook for 25–30 minutes until they brown. Put the browned bones, carrots and onions into a large pan and add the water. Bring slowly to the boil, removing all the scum that rises to the surface.
Add the remaining ingredients. Bring back to the boil, cover and simmer for 3 hours. Strain through muslin or a fine sieve before using.
Makes 1.75 litres/3 pints

Minestra di cavoli
Cabbage and bacon soup

Metric
2 × 15 ml spoons olive oil
1 large onion, peeled and
  finely chopped
100 g fat bacon, diced
1 × 2.5 ml spoon chilli
  powder
1 garlic clove, peeled and
  crushed
1 small green cabbage,
  finely shredded
1 litre Brodo di Manzo
  (see left)
2 × 15 ml spoons chopped
  fresh parsley
salt
freshly ground black pepper

Imperial
2 tablespoons olive oil
1 large onion, peeled and
  finely chopped
4 oz fat bacon, diced
½ teaspoon chilli
  powder
1 garlic clove, peeled and
  crushed
1 small green cabbage,
  finely shredded
1¾ pints Brodo di Manzo
  (see left)
2 tablespoons chopped fresh
  parsley
salt
freshly ground black pepper

Preparation time: 3 minutes
Cooking time: 35–40 minutes

Chilli powder is very hot, so it is wise to use it cautiously.

Heat the oil in a pan and fry the onion with the fat bacon for 3–4 minutes. Stir in the chilli powder and cook for 1 minute. Add the garlic and shredded cabbage and cook for a further 5 minutes. Stir in the remaining ingredients. Bring to the boil, cover and simmer for 25–30 minutes.

Minestra di cavoli

Minestra di ceci
Chick pea soup

Metric	Imperial
225 g dried chick peas	8 oz dried chick peas
salt	salt
generous pinch of bicarbonate of soda	generous pinch of bicarbonate of soda
4 × 15 ml spoons olive oil	4 tablespoons olive oil
1 large onion, peeled and sliced	1 large onion, peeled and sliced
1 small head fennel, thinly sliced	1 small head fennel, thinly sliced
freshly ground black pepper	freshly ground black pepper
1 × 100 g piece prosciutto or other Parma ham, cut into strips	1 × 4 oz piece prosciutto or other Parma ham, cut into strips

Preparation time: 35 minutes, plus standing
Cooking time: 2 hours 40 minutes

Although the preparation of this soup may seem rather fiddly, the method used does actually reduce the cooking time of the chick peas – they usually take 5–6 hours.

Put the chick peas into a large bowl with a handful of salt and sufficient warm water to cover them well. Leave to stand for 24 hours.
Drain the peas. Bring 2.25 litres/4 pints water to the boil. Add the bicarbonate of soda and the drained chick peas and simmer for 1 hour. Drain the chick peas once again, discarding the liquid. Put the chick peas into a clean pan with 1.75 litres/3 pints lightly salted water. Bring to the boil, cover and simmer for 45 minutes. Drain the chick peas, reserving their cooking liquid.
Heat the oil in a large pan and gently fry the onion for 5 minutes. Add the sliced fennel and continue cooking for a further 5 minutes. Add the drained chick peas, salt and pepper to taste, and the reserved cooking liquid. Cover and simmer for 45 minutes, or until the peas are soft.
Either push the soup through a sieve or blend in a liquidizer. Return the soup to the pan, adding the chopped ham, and heat through. The soup may be thinned with a little stock or water if preferred. Serve piping hot with fried bread croûtons.
Serves 4–6

Brodetto di ancona
Fish and saffron soup

Metric	Imperial
1 kg assorted fish, cleaned (cod, skate, prawns, red mullet, squid)	2 lb assorted fish, cleaned (cod, skate, prawns, red mullet, squid)
flour	flour
6 × 15 ml spoons olive oil	6 tablespoons olive oil
1 large onion, peeled and thinly sliced	1 large onion, peeled and thinly sliced
450 ml water	¾ pint water
450 ml dry white wine	¾ pint dry white wine
generous pinch of saffron, soaked in a little warm water	generous pinch of saffron, soaked in a little warm water
1–2 × 15 ml spoons white wine vinegar	1–2 tablespoons white wine vinegar
salt	salt
freshly ground black pepper	freshly ground black pepper
4 small slices crusty bread	4 small slices crusty bread
2 garlic cloves, peeled	2 garlic cloves, peeled

Preparation time: 30 minutes
Cooking time: 35 minutes

Although this soup has a better flavour if a variety of fish is used, you can use just two or three of those listed above.

Cut the cod and skate into large chunks; remove the heads from the prawns, and any eggs; remove the heads and tails from the mullet, and cut into large chunks. To clean the squid pull the head part gently but firmly away from the body. Remove the hard transparent bone. Peel off the purplish red veil of skin from the body. Rinse the squid body in cold salted water, removing the milky white entrails inside. Cut into rings. Dip all the prepared fish into flour to give a thin even coating.
Heat the oil in a large pan and gently fry the onion until soft. Add the squid and mullet, and cook for 5 minutes. Add the skate and cod, and cook for a further 5 minutes. Add the prawns, water, wine, saffron liquid, vinegar, and salt and pepper to taste. Cover and simmer for 20 minutes.
Meanwhile, rub the bread with the cut garlic. Put a piece of bread into each soup bowl and spoon the fish and its liquid on top. Serve immediately.

From the back, clockwise: Minestra di ceci;
Zuppa alla pasqualina; Brodetto di ancona

Zuppa alla pasqualina
Easter onion soup

Metric
2 × 15 ml spoons olive oil
25 g butter
4 large onions (about
   750 g), peeled and thinly
   sliced
1 litre Brodo di Manzo
   (page 9)
2 garlic cloves, peeled and
   crushed
salt
freshly ground black pepper
3 egg yolks
4 × 15 ml spoons Grappa
   or other brandy

Imperial
2 tablespoons olive oil
1 oz butter
4 large onions (about
   1½ lb), peeled and
   thinly sliced
1¾ pints Brodo di Manzo
   (page 9)
2 garlic cloves, peeled and
   crushed
salt
freshly ground black pepper
3 egg yolks
4 tablespoons Grappa or
   other brandy

Preparation time: 5 minutes
Cooking time: 40–45 minutes

The fiery Italian brandy, Grappa, is traditionally used in this soup, but any brandy will give the soup a good, full-bodied flavour.

Heat the oil and butter in a large pan and gently fry the onions over a moderate heat until they start to soften. Cover and cook gently for 20 minutes. Add the Brodo di Manzo, garlic, and salt and pepper to taste. Simmer for 10 minutes. Beat the egg yolks with the brandy and blend in a little of the soup. Return this mixture to the pan and stir over the heat for 1 minute – the soup must not be allowed to boil. Serve immediately with warm crusty bread.

Pasta e fagioli
Pasta and bean soup

Metric	Imperial
150 g dried white beans, soaked overnight	5 oz dried white beans, soaked overnight
4 × 15 ml spoons olive oil	4 tablespoons olive oil
1 medium onion, peeled and finely chopped	1 medium onion, peeled and finely chopped
2 carrots, peeled and chopped	2 carrots, peeled and chopped
2 sticks celery, finely chopped	2 sticks celery, finely chopped
1.75 litres Brodo di Pollo (page 8)	3 pints Brodo di Pollo (page 8)
1 garlic clove, peeled and crushed	1 garlic clove, peeled and crushed
salt	salt
freshly ground black pepper	freshly ground black pepper
75 g pasta shells	3 oz pasta shells
50 g grated Parmesan cheese (optional)	2 oz grated Parmesan cheese (optional)

Preparation time: 10–15 minutes, plus soaking
Cooking time: 2¾ hours

Drain the beans. Heat the oil in a pan and gently fry the onion, carrots and celery for 5 minutes.
Add the Brodo di Pollo, beans, garlic and salt and pepper to taste. Bring to the boil, cover and simmer for 2 hours.
Remove about half the beans from the soup, and either push through a sieve or blend in a liquidizer. Add the bean purée to the soup. Bring the soup back to the boil and add the pasta. Cook steadily for a further 8–10 minutes until the pasta is tender. Serve in soup bowls sprinkled with grated Parmesan cheese, if using.

Pasta e fagioli; Minestra di funghi; Minestra di pomodoro

Minestra di funghi
Lentil and dried mushroom soup

Metric	Imperial
175 g lentils, preferably brown	6 oz lentils, preferably brown
75 g fat Parma ham, diced	3 oz fat Parma ham, diced
1 large onion, peeled and thinly sliced	1 large onion, peeled and thinly sliced
4 tomatoes, skinned and roughly chopped	4 tomatoes, skinned and roughly chopped
2 garlic cloves, peeled and crushed	2 garlic cloves, peeled and crushed
2 sticks celery, finely chopped	2 sticks celery, finely chopped
1 × 15 ml spoon chopped fresh mint	1 tablespoon chopped fresh mint
salt	salt
freshly ground black pepper	freshly ground black pepper
1.75 litres Brodo di Manzo (page 9)	3 pints Brodo di Manzo (page 9)
25 g dried mushrooms	1 oz dried mushrooms

Preparation time: 35 minutes, plus soaking
Cooking time: 1 hour 20 minutes

Dried mushrooms have a very subtle flavour, which is destroyed if the mushrooms are overcooked.

Soak the lentils in cold water for 4 hours. Put the ham into a pan and stir over a gentle heat until the fat starts to run. Add the onion and fry gently for 5 minutes. Add the tomatoes, garlic, celery and mint, and gently fry for a further 5 minutes. Add the drained lentils, salt and pepper to taste, and the Brodo di Manzo. Bring to the boil, cover and simmer for 1 hour. Meanwhile, soak the dried mushrooms in tepid water for 30 minutes. Drain the mushrooms and slice them. Add the mushrooms to the soup, and continue cooking for a further 8 minutes.

Minestra di pomodoro
Iced tomato and basil soup

Metric	Imperial
1 kg tomatoes, skinned, seeded and chopped	2 lb tomatoes, skinned, seeded and chopped
4 × 15 ml spoons olive oil	4 tablespoons olive oil
1 garlic clove, peeled and crushed	1 garlic clove, peeled and crushed
1 × 15 ml spoon chopped fresh basil	1 tablespoon chopped fresh basil
generous pinch of sugar	generous pinch of sugar
600 ml Brodo di Pollo (page 8)	1 pint Brodo di Pollo (page 8)
salt	salt
freshly ground black pepper	freshly ground black pepper

Crostini:	Crostini:
4 anchovy fillets	4 anchovy fillets
4 small slices crusty bread	4 small slices crusty bread
1 large garlic clove, peeled	1 large garlic clove, peeled
4 × 15 ml spoons olive oil	4 tablespoons olive oil
4 slices Bel Paese cheese	4 slices Bel Paese cheese

Preparation time: 30 minutes, plus chilling
Cooking time: 25–30 minutes
Oven: 190°C, 375°F, Gas Mark 5

Put the tomatoes and oil into a pan. Cover and cook gently for 10 minutes. Add the garlic, basil, sugar, Brodo di Pollo, and salt and pepper to taste. Cook gently for a further 5 minutes. Blend the soup in a liquidizer until smooth. Chill for 4–6 hours.
To make the Crostini, soak the anchovy fillets in warm water for 10 minutes to remove the excess salt. Split each anchovy fillet in two. Rub the slices of bread with the cut garlic, and brush with olive oil. Top each slice of bread with a slice of cheese and arrange on a baking sheet. Place in a preheated oven and bake for 10–15 minutes until crisp and lightly golden. Top each crostini with a criss-cross of anchovy fillets. Serve hot as a garnish with bowls of the chilled soup.

STARTERS

A display of Italian hors d'oeuvre is as colourful as a painter's palette – sardines glisten with olive oil; slices of Parma ham, so paper thin that you can almost see through them; shiny strips of pickled yellow and red peppers; rings of squid in a herb dressing; and baby mushrooms in a chilled tomato and garlic sauce. These are just a few simple varieties of antipasti that are frequently offered to tickle the appetite. The secret of a good antipasti dish is that it should require very little time in the kitchen to prepare, and that it should win over the eater with the first bite. Not all the recipes in this section are necessarily quick to prepare, but those that take a little longer are well worth the effort.

San Daniele con ricotta; Funghi alla toscana; Insalata di fagioli

San Daniele con ricotta
Ham with cheese and herb filling

Metric	Imperial
225 g Ricotta or curd cheese	*8 oz Ricotta or curd cheese*
2 × 5 ml spoons Pesto sauce (page 40)	*2 teaspoons Pesto sauce (page 40)*
6 large black olives, stoned and chopped	*6 large black olives, stoned and chopped*
salt	*salt*
freshly ground black pepper	*freshly ground black pepper*
8 thin slices San Daniele, or any other good ham (see page 7)	*8 thin slices San Daniele, or any other good ham (see page 7)*
3 × 15 ml spoons olive oil	*3 tablespoons olive oil*
8 black olives, to garnish	*8 black olives, to garnish*

Preparation time: 15–20 minutes

Mix the Ricotta or curd cheese with the Pesto, chopped olives, and salt and pepper to taste. Divide the mixture between the ham slices and roll up sausage fashion.
Dribble a little olive oil over each ham roll and garnish with black olives. Serve with crusty bread.

Funghi alla toscana
Mushrooms in tomato sauce

Metric	Imperial
6 × 15 ml spoons olive oil	6 tablespoons olive oil
1 onion, peeled and finely chopped	1 onion, peeled and finely chopped
450 g tomatoes, skinned, seeded and chopped	1 lb tomatoes, skinned, seeded and chopped
2 garlic cloves, peeled and crushed	2 garlic cloves, peeled and crushed
1 × 15 ml spoons chopped fresh oregano	1 tablespoon chopped fresh oregano
salt	salt
freshly ground black pepper	freshly ground black pepper
275 g small button mushrooms	10 oz small button mushrooms

Preparation time: 5 minutes, plus chilling
Cooking time: 30 minutes

Although fresh oregano gives the best flavour to this dish, you can use 1 × 5 ml spoon/1 teaspoon dried oregano in its place.

Heat half the oil in a large shallow pan and gently fry the onion for 5 minutes. Add the tomatoes, garlic, oregano, and salt and pepper to taste. Simmer gently for 10 minutes.
Add the button mushrooms and cook gently in the sauce for about 6 minutes until the mushrooms are just tender. Remove the pan from the heat, stir in the remaining oil and transfer to a shallow serving dish. Chill for 3–4 hours.

Insalata di fagioli
Red bean salad

Metric	Imperial
225 g dried red kidney beans, soaked overnight	8 oz dried red kidney beans, soaked overnight
150 ml olive oil	¼ pint olive oil
grated rind and juice of ½ lemon	grated rind and juice of ½ lemon
salt	salt
freshly ground black pepper	freshly ground black pepper
1 garlic clove, peeled and crushed	1 garlic clove, peeled and crushed
1 large onion, peeled and thinly sliced	1 large onion, peeled and thinly sliced
1 medium yellow pepper, cored, seeded and finely chopped	1 medium yellow pepper, cored, seeded and finely chopped
175 g salami, in one piece, cut into small cubes or strips	6 oz salami, in one piece, cut into small cubes or strips
2 × 15 ml spoons chopped fresh parsley	2 tablespoons chopped fresh parsley

Preparation time: 20 minutes, plus soaking
Cooking time: 1¾–2¼ hours

If you do not have the time to soak and cook dried beans, then use a can of red kidney beans rinsed in warm water and drained thoroughly.

Drain the beans and put into a pan with sufficient cold water to cover them well. Bring to the boil, boil rapidly for 10 minutes, then cover and simmer gently for 1½–2 hours, until the beans are just tender.
Drain the beans thoroughly and stir in the oil while they are still warm. Add the lemon juice and rind, salt and pepper to taste, and garlic. Leave until quite cold. Stir the onion, yellow pepper, salami and parsley into the beans. Serve with a jug of olive oil and crusty bread.

Mozzarella alla griglia
Grilled mozzarella

Metric	Imperial
350 g Mozzarella cheese	*12 oz Mozzarella cheese*
olive oil	*olive oil*
freshly ground black pepper	*freshly ground black pepper*
coarse salt	*coarse salt*
1 × 15 ml spoon chopped fresh basil	*1 tablespoon chopped fresh basil*
juice of 1 lemon	*juice of 1 lemon*

Preparation time: 4–5 minutes
Cooking time: 3 minutes

This is one of the simplest of Italian starters, but quite delicious. It is very important that the griddle or frying pan is piping hot before the cheese is added, so that a golden crust forms immediately. To test that the pan is hot enough, cut off a small corner of cheese and drop into the pan. It should sizzle and colour immediately on contact with the hot oil.

Cut the cheese into 1 cm/½ inch thick slices. Lightly grease a griddle or solid-based frying pan with oil and heat until it is very hot. Add the cheese slices and as soon as they colour on the underside, flip them over with a spatula. Continue cooking until the cheese has a good crust on the other side.
Put on to small plates and serve immediately sprinkled with a little extra olive oil, pepper, salt, basil and lemon juice.

Insalata di fave
Broad bean and cheese salad

Metric	Imperial
1 kg young broad beans, unshelled weight, shelled	*2 lb young broad beans, unshelled weight, shelled*
150 ml good quality green olive oil	*¼ pint good quality green olive oil*
2 garlic cloves, peeled and crushed	*2 garlic cloves, peeled and crushed*
salt	*salt*
freshly ground black pepper	*freshly ground black pepper*
2 × 15 ml spoons chopped fresh sage	*2 tablespoons chopped fresh sage*
100 g Pecorino cheese, crumbled	*4 oz Pecorino cheese, crumbled*

Preparation time: 15 minutes, plus chilling

There are several varieties of Pecorino cheese, but all are made from sheeps' milk and have a slightly sharp flavour, somewhat similar to Parmesan. This salad is equally good if it is made without the cheese.

Put the broad beans into a bowl. Add the olive oil, garlic, salt and pepper to taste, and half the sage. Stir the dressing into the beans so that they are evenly coated. Cover the bowl and chill for 2 hours.
Just before serving, stir in the crumbled cheese and sprinkle with the remaining sage.
Serves 4–6

Mozzarella alla griglia; Insalata di fave; Bruschetta; Peperoni gratinati

Bruschetta
Garlic and herb 'toast'

Metric
150 ml good quality olive
    oil
4 garlic cloves, peeled and
    crushed
3 × 15 ml spoons chopped
    fresh parsley
salt
freshly ground black pepper
4 thick slices crusty bread

Imperial
¼ pint good quality olive
    oil
4 garlic cloves, peeled and
    crushed
3 tablespoons chopped fresh
    parsley
salt
freshly ground black pepper
4 thick slices crusty bread

Preparation time: 5 minutes
Cooking time: 3 minutes

Bruschetta is frequently eaten by the olive-pickers at harvest time, as they consider the first-pressing oil to be the best to use for this dish. An equally good alternative to Bruschetta can be made by spreading slices of bread generously with Pesto sauce (page 40), and then grilling them.

Mix the olive oil with the garlic, parsley, and salt and pepper to taste. Dip both sides of each slice of bread into the flavoured oil and place on a baking sheet. Place under a preheated hot grill, turning once, until crisp and golden. Spoon over any flavoured oil that remains before serving.
Alternatively, the Bruschetta can be baked in a preheated moderately hot oven.

Peperoni gratinati
Stuffed baked peppers

Metric
4 small peppers
1 × 400 g can tomatoes,
    drained
1 garlic clove, peeled and
    crushed
salt
freshly ground black pepper
1 × 15 ml spoon finely
    chopped fresh rosemary
175 g Mozzarella cheese,
    cubed
6 anchovy fillets, chopped
2 × 15 ml spoons grated
    Parmesan cheese
8 × 15 ml spoons olive oil

Imperial
4 small peppers
1 × 14 oz can tomatoes,
    drained
1 garlic clove, peeled and
    crushed
salt
freshly ground black pepper
1 tablespoon finely chopped
    fresh rosemary
6 oz Mozzarella cheese,
    cubed
6 anchovy fillets, chopped
2 tablespoons grated
    Parmesan cheese
8 tablespoons olive oil

Preparation time: 20 minutes, plus chilling
Cooking time: 30–35 minutes
Oven: 190°C, 375°F, Gas Mark 5

Cut a thin slice from the stalk end of each pepper. Remove the seeds. Stand the peppers closely together in a small ovenproof dish, so that they remain upright. Mix all the remaining ingredients together, except the olive oil. Fill each pepper with the cheese and tomato mixture. Spoon over half the oil. Place the peppers in a preheated oven and bake for 30–35 minutes. Remove the peppers from the oven, spoon over the remaining oil and chill for 2–3 hours.

Insalata di cozze
Mussel salad

Metric	Imperial
2.25 litres mussels	4 pints mussels
300 ml dry white wine	1/2 pint dry white wine
2 × 15 ml spoons chopped fresh basil	2 tablespoons chopped fresh basil
2 egg yolks	2 egg yolks
juice of 1/2 lemon	juice of 1/2 lemon
200 ml olive oil	1/3 pint olive oil
2 garlic cloves, peeled and crushed	2 garlic cloves, peeled and crushed
1 × 15 ml spoon chopped fresh parlsey	1 tablespoons chopped fresh parsley
salt	salt
freshly ground black pepper	freshly ground black pepper

Preparation time: 30 minutes, plus chilling
Cooking time: 5 minutes

Scrub the mussels with a stiff brush under cold running water, discarding any that have damaged shells. If any are open, tap them sharply and if they do not close, discard them. Put the cleaned mussels into a large pan with the wine and 1 × 15 ml spoon/1 tablespoon of the basil. Cook, covered, over a moderate heat for about 5 minutes until the shells open. Discard any mussels that fail to open. Strain off the liquid from the mussels and reserve.
Open the mussels, detaching one shell and leaving each mussel on its half shell. Arrange the mussels on a shallow serving dish.
Put the egg yolks into a bowl and beat in the lemon juice. Whisk in the oil in a fine trickle, as if making mayonnaise. Add the garlic, parsley, salt and pepper to taste, and the remaining basil. Add sufficient of the strained cooking liquid to the sauce to give a thin pouring consistency. Pour the sauce evenly over the mussels. Chill for 2–3 hours. Serve with crusty bread.

Scampi alla griglia
Skewered prawns

Metric	Imperial
20 giant prawns	20 giant prawns
150 ml olive oil	1/4 pint olive oil
4 × 15 ml spoons white wine	4 tablespoons white wine
1 bay leaf, crushed	1 bay leaf, crushed
1 × 15 ml spoons chopped fresh basil	1 tablespoon chopped fresh basil
2 × 15 ml spoons chopped fresh parsley	2 tablespoons chopped fresh parsley
salt	salt
freshly ground black pepper	freshly ground black pepper
1 garlic clove, peeled and crushed	1 garlic clove, peeled and crushed
Bagna Cauda sauce (page 44)	Bagna Cauda sauce (page 44)

Preparation time: 20 minutes, plus chilling
Cooking time: 6–8 minutes

Giant prawns are not always readily available, so the standard size prawns can be used instead – allow 8 or 9 per person. Keep the marinade in a screw top jar in the refrigerator, as it can be used again.

Remove the heads from the prawns, and any eggs – otherwise leave the prawns intact. Put them into a shallow dish. Mix the olive oil with the wine, herbs, salt and pepper to taste, and garlic. Pour the marinade over the prawns. Cover and chill for 4–6 hours.
Remove the prawns from their marinade and thread on to skewers – 5 prawns per skewer. Put on the rack of a grill pan and brush with the marinade. Place under a preheated hot grill for 3–4 minutes. Turn the skewers and brush the prawns with Bagna Cauda sauce. Grill for a further 3–4 minutes. Serve hot with a bowl of hot Bagna Cauda sauce.

Crostini fritto di mare
Clam and prawn toasts

Preparation time: 15–20 minutes
Cooking time: 8–9 minutes

Metric
1 can shelled clams, 150 g
   drained weight
100 g peeled prawns
salt
freshly ground black pepper
plain flour
100 g butter
3 × 15 ml spoons olive oil
3 slices bread, crusts
   removed
1 garlic clove, peeled and
   crushed
2 × 15 ml spoons chopped
   fresh parsley
6 lemon wedges, to serve

Imperial
1 can shelled clams, 5 oz
   drained weight
4 oz peeled prawns
salt
freshly ground black pepper
plain flour
4 oz butter
3 tablespoons olive oil
3 slices bread, crusts
   removed
1 garlic clove, peeled and
   crushed
2 tablespoons chopped fresh
   parsley
6 lemon wedges, to serve

If clams are difficult to obtain, then use cockles – most supermarkets sell them in small glass jars. Rinse and drain them well as they are usually preserved in brine.

Season the clams and peeled prawns with salt and pepper, then roll them in the flour. Heat half the butter in a large shallow pan with the olive oil. Cut each slice of bread in half. Add the rectangles of bread to the hot fat and fry until lightly golden on both sides. Drain the pieces of fried bread and keep warm.
Add the remaining butter to the pan, together with the crushed garlic. Add the floured shellfish and fry gently for 4–5 minutes. Spoon on to the pieces of fried bread, sprinkle with chopped parsley and serve hot with lemon wedges.
Serves 6

Insalata di cozze; Scampi alla griglia;
Crostini fritto di mare

Supplì
Deep fried rice balls

Metric
450 g cooked Risotto alla
  Milanese (page 30)
3 eggs
salt
freshly ground black pepper
100 g Mozzarella or Bel
  Paese cheese, cut into
  1 cm cubes
1 slice Mortadella, 1 cm
  thick, cut into small
  cubes
flour
75 g fine breadcrumbs
oil for deep frying

Imperial
1 lb cooked Risotto alla
  Milanese (page 30)
3 eggs
salt
freshly ground black pepper
4 oz Mozzarella or Bel
  Paese cheese, cut into ½
  inch cubes
1 slice Mortadella, ½ inch
  thick, cut into small
  cubes
flour
3 oz fine breadcrumbs
oil for deep frying

Preparation time: 30–35 minutes, plus chilling
Cooking time: 5 minutes

The Italians fondly refer to these rice and cheese balls
as 'Suppli al Telefono' (telephone wires) – when they
are cooked and pulled in half, the cheese in the centre
forms thin strands.

Mix the Risotto alla Milanese with two of the eggs,
lightly beaten, and add salt and pepper. Put 1 × 15 ml
spoon/1 tablespoon of the rice mixture into the palm
of one hand. Top with a cube of Mozzarella and one of
Mortadella, and finally with another 1 × 15 ml spoon/1
tablespoon of the rice mixture. Shape into a round
ball, dusting your hands with flour as you go, completely enclosing the cheese and Mortadella. Make 8–
10 balls in this way. Chill the rice balls for 1 hour.
Lightly beat the remaining egg. Dip the rice balls into
the egg and then into the breadcrumbs, rolling them to
give an even crumb coating. Lower into a pan of very
hot oil (about 190°C/375°F) and deep fry for about 5
minutes, until crisp and golden brown. Drain well on
paper towels and serve piping hot.
Serves 4–6

Crema di prosciutto
Parma ham mousse

Metric
300 ml single cream
6 × 15 ml spoons Marsala
100 g Ricotta or curd cheese
150 ml chicken stock
225 g Parma ham pieces
  and 2–3 slices Parma
  ham (see below)
15 g powdered gelatine
3 × 15 ml spoons hot water

To garnish:
2 × 15 ml spoons coarsely
  chopped pistachio nuts
parsley or basil sprigs

Imperial
½ pint single cream
6 tablespoons Marsala
4 oz Ricotta or curd cheese
¼ pint chicken stock
8 oz Parma ham pieces and
  2–3 slices Parma ham
  (see below)
½ oz powdered gelatine
3 tablespoons hot water

To garnish:
2 tablespoons coarsely
  chopped pistachio nuts
parsley or basil sprigs

Preparation time: 30 minutes, plus chilling

Most delicatessens and good grocers who sell Parma
ham will sell the 'off cuts' at a very reasonable price –
these are the odd pieces that cannot be sold as full
slices. If you find Parma ham difficult to buy, then use
any well-flavoured smoked ham.

Put the cream into a liquidizer with the Marsala,
cheese, chicken stock and Parma ham pieces. Blend
until smooth. Dissolve the gelatine in the hot water
and blend into the ham mixture. The mixture has a
strong flavour and should not need additional
seasoning.
Line a lightly oiled 450 g/1 lb loaf tin with Parma ham
slices, spoon the mousse mixture in and chill for 2–3
hours until set. Turn the mousse out on to a serving
dish and garnish with the pistachio nuts and parsley or
basil. Serve with fingers of hot toast.
Serves 6

Fritata con patate; Crema di prosciutto; Supplì

Fritata con patate
Potato and sausage omelette

Preparation time: 20 minutes
Cooking time: 6 minutes

Choose either a smoked sausage or a salami for this recipe, and not a boiling sausage. It is firmer-textured than a folded omelette, as it is cooked on both sides.

Add all the ingredients, except the butter, to the beaten eggs. Melt half the butter in a large shallow omelette pan. Pour in the egg mixture and stir vigorously over a moderate heat for 1 minute. Cook, without stirring, until the underside is golden and set. Slide the omelette carefully on to a plate.

Add the remaining butter to the pan and melt over the heat. Invert the plate carefully over the the pan so that the omelette slips back into the pan, with the un-cooked side touching the bottom of the pan. Continue cooking over a moderate heat until the second side is set and golden. Transfer to a heated serving plate and serve hot, cut into wedges.

Metric	Imperial
6 eggs, lightly beaten	*6 eggs, lightly beaten*
2 medium potatoes, peeled and coarsely grated	*2 medium potatoes, peeled and coarsely grated*
salt	*salt*
freshly ground black pepper	*freshly ground black pepper*
1 garlic clove, peeled and crushed	*1 garlic clove, peeled and crushed*
1 × 15 ml spoon chopped fresh basil	*1 tablespoon chopped fresh basil*
75 g Parma ham, chopped	*3 oz Parma ham, chopped*
75 g Italian sausage, chopped	*3 oz Italian sausage, chopped*
50 g grated Parmesan cheese	*2 oz grated Parmesan cheese*
40 g butter	*1½ oz butter*

PASTA, RICE AND POLENTA

These have all been referred to as being the 'staff of Italian life', both collectively and singularly. In a way they are equivalent to the importance of the potato in this country. One of the great attributes that all three foods share is that pasta, rice and polenta dishes are relatively inexpensive to prepare – the most that they need is an accompanying sauce, and/or a sprinkling of cheese. In this section you will also find recipes for more complex dishes, such as Polenta Pasticciata and Vinci Grassi. And for those who really like 'cooking the Italian way', there is a recipe for homemade pasta dough.

Pasta all'uovo
Basic pasta dough

Metric	Imperial
450 g plain flour	*1 lb plain flour*
1 × 5 ml spoon salt	*1 teaspoon salt*
4 eggs	*4 eggs*
1 × 15 ml spoon olive oil	*1 tablespoon olive oil*
extra flour for rolling	*extra flour for rolling*

Preparation time: 30 minutes, plus relaxing

Homemade pasta is not difficult to make, but it does require patience and time. People who have a gift for making pastry and bread will have very little problem in making pasta, as many of the skills applied to all 3 are the same. The most important thing to remember is that you need plenty of uncluttered work surface – a very large chopping board or marble slab is ideal, but the modern laminate work tops are perfectly adequate. An extra large rolling pin will make the rolling of the pasta dough much easier. If you plan to go into pasta making in a big way then it may be worth your while to buy a pasta machine – at the turn of a handle you can cut many different shapes and thicknesses of pasta. These machines are now widely available in specialist kitchenware shops.

Pasta all'uovo

Sift the flour and salt into a mound on a clean work surface, and make a hollow in the centre. Add the eggs and olive oil to the hollow in the flour. Break up the eggs with the fingers, then work the flour into the eggs until you have a smooth dough. Knead the dough on a floured surface until it is firm, smooth and elastic – this will take about 10 minutes. Wring out a cloth in warm water. Wrap the dough in the cloth and leave to relax for 30 minutes.

Divide the dough into two equal portions. Roll each portion of dough out on a lightly floured surface, lifting the dough occasionally between rolling, until it is paper thin – you should be able to hold the dough up and see dark objects through it. The pasta dough is now ready to use for fettuccine, lasagne, or ravioli.

If you are making ravioli (page 24), use the rolled dough immediately; for fettuccine and lasagne, hang the rolled sheets of pasta dough over a clean cloth on the back of a chair, and leave to 'dry' for 10 minutes. To shape fettuccine and tagliatelle, roll the sheets of pasta dough up loosely, as for a Swiss roll. For fettuccine, cut through at just under 5 mm/¼ inch intervals, to form long narrow strips. Cut double the thickness for tagliatelle. Gently unroll the pasta strips with a light tossing movement, to prevent the strips from sticking together. The fettuccine can be cooked immediately, or hung over a lightly floured cloth to dry. The dried fettuccine can be lightly wrapped in waxed paper and stored in the refrigerator for up to 24 hours. It can also be frozen successfully wrapped in kitchen foil.

When cooking homemade fettuccine, it is worth remembering that all homemade pasta takes far less time to cook than manufactured packeted pasta. Lower the fettuccine into a large pan of rapidly boiling salted water and cook for 3–4 minutes. The fettuccine will rise to the surface when it is ready. Drain well and toss in melted butter with salt and freshly ground black pepper to taste. Serve with grated Parmesan cheese or any of the accompanying sauces suggested on pages 40–45.
Serves 4–6

Variation:
Pasta Verde: cook 100 g/4 oz washed and drained spinach, without any additional water, until tender. Drain the spinach thoroughly, squeezing out all the liquid. Push the cooked spinach through a sieve. Make up the Basic Pasta Dough as above, adding the spinach purée to the dry ingredients with only 3 eggs. Roll and shape in the same way. Pasta verde can be used to make a delicious homemade lasagne. Roll the green pasta dough out into sheets as for the basic homemade pasta, and hang to dry for 20 minutes. Cut into rectangles 7.5 × 15 cm/3 × 6 inches. Cook in boiling salted water for 4 minutes or until the lasagne strips rise to the surface. Drain the lasagne and lay out in separate sheets on a wet tea towel. Use in place of manufactured pasta in any made-up lasagne recipe.

Ravioli di pesce
Fish ravioli

Metric	Imperial
225 g cooked white fish, flaked	8 oz cooked white fish, flaked
25 g grated Parmesan cheese	1 oz grated Parmesan cheese
grated rind and juice of ½ lemon	grated rind and juice of ½ lemon
1 egg yolk	1 egg yolk
salt	salt
freshly ground black pepper	freshly ground black pepper
generous pinch of grated nutmeg	generous pinch of grated nutmeg
1 × 5 ml spoon anchovy paste	1 teaspoon anchovy paste
Pasta all'Uovo (page 23)	Pasta all'Uovo (page 23)
Salsa di Pomodoro e Basilico (page 44)	Salsa di Pomodoro e Basilico (page 44)
extra grated Parmesan cheese, to serve	extra grated Parmesan cheese, to serve

Preparation time: 35 minutes
Cooking time: 5–6 minutes

There are special shaped moulds available for making ravioli, but these are by no means essential when making ravioli at home. Ravioli needs to be shaped and cut quite quickly, before the pasta dough has a chance to dry and crack.

Mix the flaked fish with the Parmesan cheese, lemon rind and juice, egg yolk, salt and pepper to taste, nutmeg and anchovy paste. Roll out the prepared pasta dough into 4 thin even-sized rectangles. Place small mounds of fish filling 4 cm/1½ inches apart in straight lines on two sheets of the pasta dough. Run a dampened pastry brush in straight lines in between.
Lay the two remaining sheets of pasta dough over the top of those with the fish filling. Press down firmly between each mound of filling, to seal the two layers of pasta dough together. Run a pastry wheel or sharp knife in straight lines, following the pressed channels that you have made, so as to cut the ravioli into 5 cm/2 inch squares. Separate the squares and put on to a clean floured cloth.
Bring a large pan of salted water to the boil and drop in the ravioli. Cook for 5–6 minutes until the ravioli have risen to the surface. Remove the cooked ravioli with a slotted spoon, draining them well, and put into a heated serving dish. Spoon hot Salsa di Pomodoro e Basilico over the ravioli and sprinkle with grated Parmesan cheese. Serve extra Parmesan cheese separately in a bowl.
Serves 6

Vinci grassi
Lasagne with meatballs

Metric	Imperial
225 g lean beef, finely minced	8 oz lean beef, finely minced
175 g Parma ham, finely minced	6 oz Parma ham, finely minced
1 small onion, peeled and grated	1 small onion, peeled and grated
1 × 15 ml spoon chopped fresh sage	1 tablespoon chopped fresh sage
1 garlic clove, peeled and crushed	1 garlic clove, peeled and crushed
salt	salt
freshly ground black pepper	freshly ground black pepper
2 egg yolks	2 egg yolks
oil for frying	oil for frying
900 ml Besciamella (page 45)	1½ pints Besciamella (page 45)
175 g Mozzarella or Bel Paese cheese, diced	6 oz Mozzarella or Bel Paese cheese, diced
225 g lasagne	8 oz lasagne
4 × 15 ml spoons grated Parmesan cheese	4 tablespoons grated Parmesan cheese

Preparation time: 25–30 minutes
Cooking time: about 45 minutes, depending on type of lasagne
Oven: 180°C, 350°F, Gas Mark 4

Mix the minced meats with the onion, sage, garlic, salt and pepper to taste, and the egg yolks. Form into small meatballs, about the size of a large olive. Shallow fry the meatballs in oil until lightly browned on all sides. Drain on paper towels. Mix the Besciamella with the diced cheese.
Lower the lasagne into a large pan of boiling salted water, adding one sheet at a time. Cook at a steady rolling boil – 4 minutes for homemade lasagne, 10–12 minutes for packet lasagne. Drain the cooked lasagne and lay out in single sheets on a wet tea towel. This will prevent the lasagne from sticking.
Put a little of the Besciamella into the base of a greased large shallow rectangular ovenproof dish. Add a layer of lasagne, a few meatballs, and a little more of the sauce. Continue with alternate layers of lasagne, meatballs and sauce, finishing with a layer of sauce. Sprinkle with the grated Parmesan cheese. Place in a preheated oven and bake for 35–40 minutes until golden and bubbling.
Serve hot.
Serves 4–6

Ravioli di pesce; Vinci grassi

Pasta alla carrettiera
Macaroni with spicy olive sauce

Metric	Imperial
450 g penne (diagonally-cut macaroni)	1 lb penne (diagonally-cut macaroni)
salt	salt
8 × 15 ml spoons olive oil	8 tablespoons olive oil
1 × 2.5 ml spoon ground ginger	½ teaspoon ground ginger
generous pinch of grated nutmeg	generous pinch of grated nutmeg
freshly ground black pepper	freshly ground black pepper
1 garlic clove, peeled and crushed	1 garlic clove, peeled and crushed
3 × 15 ml spoons capers	3 tablespoons capers
75 g stoned black olives, sliced	3 oz stoned black olives, sliced
2 × 15 ml spoons chopped fresh parsley	2 tablespoons chopped fresh parsley

Preparation time: 3 minutes
Cooking time: 11–12 minutes

Cook the macaroni in boiling salted water for 10 minutes. Drain thoroughly. Return the cooked macaroni to the pan, together with the oil, ginger, nutmeg, pepper, garlic, capers, olives and parsley. Stir over a gentle heat for 1–2 minutes. Serve immediately.
Serves 4–6

Lasagne con gamberetti
Mussel and prawn lasagne

Metric	Imperial
225 g lasagne	8 oz lasagne
salt	salt
600 ml Salsa di Pomodoro (page 44)	1 pint Salsa di Pomodoro (page 44)
2 × 15 ml spoons chopped fresh parsley	2 tablespoons chopped fresh parsley
175 g shelled mussels	6 oz shelled mussels
175 g peeled prawns	6 oz peeled prawns
6 canned artichoke hearts, quartered	6 canned artichoke hearts, quartered
freshly ground black pepper	freshly ground black pepper
100 g Mozzarella cheese, thinly sliced	4 oz Mozzarella cheese, thinly sliced
6 anchovy fillets, split lengthways	6 anchovy fillets, split lengthways

Preparation time: 10 minutes
Cooking time: about 40 minutes, depending on type of lasagne
Oven: 180°C, 350°F, Gas Mark 4

Lower the lasagne into a large pan of boiling salted water, adding one sheet at a time. Cook at a steady rolling boil – 4 minutes for homemade lasagne, 10–12 minutes for packet lasagne. Drain the cooked lasagne and lay out in single sheets on a wet tea towel. This will prevent the lasagne from sticking.
Put a little of the Salsa di Pomodoro into the base of a greased large shallow rectangular ovenproof dish. Add a layer of lasagne. Mix the remaining Salsa di Pomodoro with the parsley, mussels, prawns, artichoke hearts, and salt and pepper to taste. Alternate layers of sauce and lasagne, finishing with a layer of sauce. Top with the sliced Mozzarella cheese and a criss-cross of anchovy fillets. Place in a preheated oven and bake for 35–40 minutes until golden and bubbling.
Serve hot.
Serves 4–6

Vermicelli siciliana
Vermicelli with aubergines

Metric	Imperial
4 × 15 ml spoons olive oil	4 tablespoons olive oil
1 medium onion, peeled and finely chopped	1 medium onion, peeled and finely chopped
750 g tomatoes, skinned, seeded and chopped	1½ lb tomatoes, skinned, seeded and chopped
2 × 15 ml spoons tomato purée	2 tablespoons tomato purée
150 ml red wine	¼ pint red wine
1 large aubergine, chopped	1 large aubergine, chopped
1 large red pepper, cored, seeded and finely chopped	1 large red pepper, cored, seeded and finely chopped
1 large green pepper, cored, seeded and finely chopped	1 large green pepper, cored, seeded and finely chopped
8 anchovy fillets, chopped	8 anchovy fillets, chopped
1 garlic clove, peeled and crushed	1 garlic clove, peeled and crushed
450 g vermicelli	1 lb vermicelli
salt	salt
75 g black olives (tiny ones)	3 oz black olives (tiny ones)
freshly ground black pepper	freshly ground black pepper

Preparation time: 3 minutes
Cooking time: 23 minutes

Vermicelli cooks much more quickly than most other varieties of packeted pasta, and great care is needed so as not to overcook it. Vermicelli can be bought in several different forms – in straight lengths, like a thin spaghetti; folded, like a skein of wool; and in nest-shaped clusters. It does not matter which variety you use in this recipe.

Heat the oil in a pan and gently fry the onion for 3 minutes. Add the chopped tomato, tomato purée, red wine, aubergine, peppers, anchovy fillets and garlic. Simmer gently for 20 minutes.
Cook the vermicelli in a large pan of boiling salted water for 2–3 minutes until tender. Drain the cooked vermicelli thoroughly and toss in the prepared sauce, adding the black olives and salt and pepper to taste. Serve immediately.
Serves 4–6

Pasta alla carrettiera; Lasagne con gamberetti; Vermicelli siciliana

Fettuccine calabrese
Noodles with ham sauce

Metric	Imperial
4 × 15 ml spoons olive oil	4 tablespoons olive oil
1 medium onion, peeled and finely chopped	1 medium onion, peeled and finely chopped
100 g Parma ham, chopped	4 oz Parma ham, chopped
2 garlic cloves, peeled and crushed	2 garlic cloves, peeled and crushed
1 small chilli pepper, finely chopped	1 small chilli pepper, finely chopped
750 g tomatoes, skinned, seeded and chopped	1½ lb tomatoes, skinned, seeded and chopped
salt	salt
freshly ground black pepper	freshly ground black pepper
450 g fettuccine	1 lb fettuccine
75 g Pecorino cheese, grated	3 oz Pecorino cheese, grated

Preparation time: 5 minutes
Cooking time: about 15 minutes

You can either use homemade fettuccine (page 23) or the packeted dry fettuccine in this recipe. Remember that homemade fettuccine will only take 3–4 minutes to cook; the packet fettuccine will take 8–10 minutes.

Heat the olive oil in a pan and gently fry the onion for 3 minutes. Add the ham and cook for a further 2–3 minutes. Add the garlic, chilli pepper, tomatoes, and salt and pepper to taste. Cook gently for 10 minutes. Meanwhile cook the fettuccine in a large pan of boiling salted water until tender (see cooking time above). Drain the fettuccine thoroughly and toss in the tomato sauce and grated Pecorino. Serve immediately.
Serves 4–6

Pizzoccheri
Noodle and vegetable casserole

Metric	Imperial
4 × 15 ml spoons olive oil	4 tablespoons olive oil
2 onions, peeled and thinly sliced	2 onions, peeled and thinly sliced
225 g courgettes, sliced	8 oz courgettes, sliced
1 yellow pepper, cored, seeded and sliced	1 yellow pepper, cored, seeded and sliced
1 garlic clove, peeled and crushed	1 garlic clove, peeled and crushed
600 ml Salsa di Pomodoro (page 44)	1 pint Salsa di Pomodoro (page 44)
salt	salt
freshly ground black pepper	freshly ground black pepper
350 g fettuccine	12 oz fettuccine
175 g Bel Paese cheese, diced	6 oz Bel Paese cheese, diced

Preparation time: 5 minutes
Cooking time: 23 minutes
Oven: 190°C, 375°F, Gas Mark 5

Heat the oil in a pan and fry the sliced onion for 3 minutes. Add the courgettes, pepper, garlic, Salsa di Pomodoro, and salt and pepper to taste. Cover the pan and simmer for 10 minutes.
Meanwhile cook the fettuccine in boiling salted water until tender. Drain the fettuccine thoroughly and stir into the vegetable sauce, together with the diced cheese. Transfer to a casserole. Cover, place in a preheated oven and cook for 20 minutes. Serve hot.
Serves 4–6

Spaghetti alla carbonara
Spaghetti with bacon and egg

Preparation time: 5 minutes
Cooking time: 10–12 minutes

Metric
3 × 15 ml spoons olive oil
1 medium onion, peeled
   and finely chopped
350 g spaghetti
salt
6 rashers of bacon, rind
   removed, chopped
6 × 15 ml spoons dry white
   wine
4 eggs
75 g grated Parmesan
   cheese
2 × 15 ml spoons chopped
   fresh parsley
1 garlic clove, peeled
   and crushed
freshly ground black
   pepper

Imperial
3 tablespoons olive oil
1 medium onion, peeled
   and finely chopped
12 oz spaghetti
salt
6 rashers of bacon, rind
   removed, chopped
6 tablespoons dry white
   wine
4 eggs
3 oz grated Parmesan
   cheese
2 tablespoons chopped
   fresh parsley
1 garlic clove, peeled
   and crushed
freshly ground black
   pepper

Heat the oil in a pan and gently fry the onion for 5 minutes until soft. Put the spaghetti into a large pan of boiling salted water and cook for 8–10 minutes until tender. Add the chopped bacon to the onion and fry for 2 minutes, over a brisk heat. Add the wine to the bacon and onion and cook until the wine has evaporated. Beat the eggs with the grated cheese, parsley, garlic, and salt and pepper to taste.

Drain the spaghetti quickly but thoroughly. Stir in the beaten egg mixture and the bacon immediately, so that the heat from the spaghetti cooks the egg. Spoon on to hot dishes and serve immediately.

Serves 4–6

Fettuccine calabrese; Pizzoccheri; Spaghetti alla carbonara

Risotto con gamberetti
Prawn risotto

Metric	Imperial
450 g unshelled prawns	1 lb unshelled prawns
1 small head fennel	1 small head fennel
few parsley stalks	few parsley stalks
½ onion, peeled and roughly chopped	½ onion, peeled and roughly chopped
1 small carrot, peeled and roughly chopped	1 small carrot, peeled and roughly chopped
300 ml dry white wine	½ pint dry white wine
100 g butter	4 oz butter
2 × 15 ml spoons olive oil	2 tablespoons olive oil
450 g short-grain Italian rice	1 lb short-grain Italian rice
salt	salt
freshly ground black pepper	freshly ground black pepper
1 garlic clove, peeled and crushed	1 garlic clove, peeled and crushed
grated rind of ½ lemon	grated rind of ½ lemon
50 g grated Parmesan cheese	2 oz grated Parmesan cheese

Preparation time: 25 minutes
Cooking time: about 1 hour

Shell the prawns. Put the prawn shells, heads and any eggs into a pan – keep the prawns to one side. Remove the feathery tops from the fennel and reserve for garnish. Slice the bulb of fennel and add to the prawn trimmings, together with the parsley stalks, chopped onion and carrot and 1 litre/1¾ pints water. Simmer gently for 25–30 minutes. Strain the prawn stock and make up to 1.6 litres/2¾ pints with the white wine and sufficient extra water.

Heat half the butter and the oil in a pan and gently cook the rice for 5 minutes, making sure that the rice does not colour. Add a cupful of stock to the rice and cook steadily until the stock has been absorbed. Add another cup of stock and continue cooking steadily until the rice has absorbed the stock. Continue adding the stock in this way, until all the stock has been used up and the rice is tender. Add salt and pepper to taste. Melt the remaining butter in a small pan and add the peeled prawns, garlic, lemon rind and the chopped feathery tops from the fennel. Stir into the cooked risotto, together with the Parmesan cheese, and serve immediately.
Serves 4–6

Risotto alla milanese
Rice milanaise style

Metric	Imperial
1 × 2.5 ml spoon saffron	½ teaspoon saffron
3 × 15 ml spoons hot water	3 tablespoons hot water
2 × 15 ml spoons olive oil	2 tablespoons olive oil
100 g butter	4 oz butter
1 small onion, peeled and finely chopped	1 small onion, peeled and finely chopped
1 × 15 ml spoon bone marrow	1 tablespoon bone marrow
450 g short-grain Italian rice	1 lb short-grain Italian rice
150 ml dry white wine	¼ pint dry white wine
1.5 litres Brodo di Pollo (page 8)	2½ pints Brodo di Pollo (page 8)
salt	salt
freshly ground black pepper	freshly ground black pepper
50 g grated Parmesan cheese	2 oz grated Parmesan cheese

Preparation time: 3 minutes, plus soaking
Cooking time: 35 minutes

The bone marrow is not an essential ingredient, but it does add a rich quality to the risotto – ask your butcher to give you a good beef or veal bone, sawed through in such a way that it is easy to get at the marrow in the middle.

Soak the saffron in the water for 15–20 minutes. Heat the oil and half the butter in a pan and gently fry the onion for 3 minutes. Add the bone marrow and rice and stir over a gentle heat for 5 minutes, making sure that the rice does not colour. Add the white wine and cook over a brisk heat until the wine has almost evaporated.

Add a cupful of the Brodo di Pollo to the rice and cook steadily until the stock has been absorbed. Continue adding the stock in this way, until all the stock has been used up and the rice is tender – the rice should be 'creamy' and not dry. Add salt and pepper to taste, and stir in the remaining butter and the Parmesan cheese. Serve immediately.
Serves 4–6

From the back, clockwise: Risotto verde;
Risotto con gamberetti; Risotto alla milanese

Risotto verde
Risotto with spinach and herbs

Metric	Imperial
450 g spinach, fresh or frozen	1 lb spinach, fresh or frozen
2 × 15 ml spoons olive oil	2 tablespoons olive oil
100 g butter	4 oz butter
1 small onion, peeled and finely chopped	1 small onion, peeled and finely chopped
450 g short-grain Italian rice	1 lb short-grain Italian rice
1.6 litres Brodo di Pollo (page 8)	2¾ pints Brodo di Pollo (page 8)
1 × 15 ml spoon chopped fresh oregano	1 tablespoon chopped fresh oregano
1 garlic clove, peeled and crushed	1 garlic clove, peeled and crushed
salt	salt
freshly ground black pepper	freshly ground black pepper
75 g grated Parmesan cheese	3 oz grated Parmesan cheese
wedges of lemon, to garnish	wedges of lemon, to garnish

Preparation time: 5 minutes
Cooking time: 30–35 minutes

Cook the spinach in a pan, without any additional water, for 5–10 minutes until tender. Drain the spinach thoroughly and chop finely. Heat the oil and half the butter in a pan and gently fry the onion for 3 minutes. Add the rice and stir over a gentle heat for 5 minutes, making sure that the rice does not colour.
Add a cupful of the Brodo di Pollo and cook steadily until the stock has been absorbed. Add another cup of stock, the chopped spinach, oregano and garlic. Cook steadily once again until the stock has been absorbed. Continue adding the stock in this way until all the stock has been absorbed and the rice is tender. Add salt and pepper to taste and stir in the remaining butter and the Parmesan cheese. Serve immediately garnished with wedges of lemon, and accompanied by a salad.
Serves 4–6

Polenta
Semolina paste

Metric	Imperial
1 litre water	1¾ pints water
salt	salt
225 g polenta flour (fine semolina)	8 oz polenta flour (fine semolina)
freshly ground black pepper	freshly ground black pepper
butter	butter
grated Parmesan cheese	grated Parmesan cheese

Preparation time: 4–5 minutes
Cooking time: 30–35 minutes

Polenta, a sort of semolina porridge, is as popular in certain parts of Northern and Central Italy as potatoes are in this country. Sometimes it is served simply, with butter and Parmesan cheese; on other occasions it is baked with a sauce, or shaped into portions and fried. Polenta can be frozen successfully, and this is particularly useful when frying it, as in the recipe for Fegatini di Pollo (page 59). Open-freeze the shaped polenta and then pack into a freezer bag, interleaving each slice. You need to stand well back when making polenta, as it tends to spit, and it is advisable to use a long-handled wooden spoon for stirring the mixture.

Bring the water and salt to a rolling boil. Shower the polenta flour slowly but steadily into the water, stirring all the time, to prevent it hardening into solid lumps. Stir until the mixture is smooth and creamy. Lower the heat and simmer gently until the polenta is thick, but not dry – about 25–30 minutes. This gives what is called a soft polenta. Add salt and pepper to taste. Tip the cooked polenta on to a wooden serving platter and shape into a cake with a dampened spatula. Mark into sections for serving. Serve immediately topping each portion with a slice of soft butter and a generous sprinkling of Parmesan cheese.
Serves 6

Variation:
Polenta Cakes: make up the polenta as above using just under 900 ml/1½ pints water. Cook the polenta until it is really thick – about 40 minutes. Spread the polenta out on a dampened chopping board, flattening it to a thickness of 1 cm/½ inch. Cut into 7.5 cm/3 inch rounds with a pastry cutter. The polenta cakes can be coated with egg and crumbs if liked. Shallow fry in hot oil until golden on all sides. Drain and serve piping hot with Salsa di Pomodoro Crudo (page 41).

Malfatti di fontina
Gnocchi with fontina cheese

Metric	Imperial
450 g spinach, washed	1 lb spinach, washed
175 g butter	6 oz butter
salt	salt
freshly ground black pepper	freshly ground black pepper
generous pinch of grated nutmeg	generous pinch of grated nutmeg
175 g Fontina cheese, or other soft Italian cheese	6 oz Fontina cheese, or other soft Italian cheese
85 g plain flour	3 oz plain flour
1 egg	1 egg
1 egg yolk	1 egg yolk
50 g grated Parmesan cheese	2 oz grated Parmesan cheese
grated rind of 1 lemon	grated rind of 1 lemon
1 garlic clove, peeled and crushed	1 garlic clove, peeled and crushed

Preparation time: 25 minutes, plus chilling
Cooking time: 25 minutes
Oven: 200°C, 400°F, Gas Mark 6

Cook the spinach in a pan, without any additional water, for 5–10 minutes until tender. Drain well and squeeze the spinach to extract as much moisture as possible – if you have a clean piece of muslin, squeeze the cooked spinach in that. Put the spinach into a liquidizer or food processor with 25 g/1 oz of the butter, salt and pepper to taste, nutmeg, Fontina cheese, flour, whole egg and egg yolk. Blend to a smooth, soft dough. Chill the dough for 2–3 hours.
Roll out the spinach dough on a lightly floured surface to a thickness of about 8 mm/⅓ inch thickness. Stamp out into circles approximately 4 cm/1½ inches in diameter. Put the shaped gnocchi into a greased shallow ovenproof dish. Dot with half the remaining butter and sprinkle with the grated Parmesan cheese. Place in a preheated oven and bake for 15 minutes.
Meanwhile melt the remaining butter in a small pan and add the lemon rind and garlic. As soon as the gnocchi comes out of the oven, pour the flavoured butter over the top and serve immediately.
Serves 4–6

From the back, clockwise: Polenta;
Polenta pasticciata; Malfatti di fontina

Polenta pasticciata
Polenta pie

Preparation time: 10 minutes
Cooking time: 35 minutes
Oven: 200°C, 400°F, Gas Mark 6

Metric
1 quantity Polenta
  (page 32)
50 g butter
225 g mushrooms, sliced
100 g Italian salami, sliced
450 ml Besciamella
  (page 45)
salt
freshly ground black pepper
50 g grated Parmesan
  cheese

Imperial
1 quantity Polenta
  (page 32)
2 oz butter
8 oz mushrooms, sliced
4 oz Italian salami, sliced
¾ pint Besciamella
  (page 45)
salt
freshly ground black pepper
2 oz grated Parmesan
  cheese

Cook the Polenta as on page 32, but for only 20 minutes. Melt the butter in a pan and gently fry the mushrooms for 5 minutes. Spread a third of the Polenta into a greased ovenproof dish. Top with a third of the mushrooms, a third of the salami and a third of the Besciamella. Repeat these layers twice more, adding salt and pepper to taste, and finishing with a layer of sauce. Sprinkle with the Parmesan cheese. Place in a preheated oven and bake for 30 minutes. Serve piping hot.
Serves 6

PIZZAS AND PIES

A favourite snack in Roman times was 'bread with a savoury topping' – any ingredients that might make a slice of stale bread taste more palatable and look more appetizing. Eventually it occurred to someone to turn up the edges of the bread, so as to contain the topping; pizza had been invented. The variations of pizza today are limitless, and the homemade ones are without doubt the best.

Pizza
Basic pizza dough

Metric	Imperial
30 g fresh yeast or 15 g dried yeast	1 oz fresh yeast or ½ oz dried yeast
300 ml tepid water	½ pint tepid water
450 g plain flour	1 lb plain flour
1 × 2.5 ml spoon salt	½ teaspoon salt

Preparation time: 25 minutes, plus rising

This quantity of basic pizza dough will make one large pizza, to serve 4–6 people, or four individual pizzas.

Crumble the fresh yeast into a small bowl. Add half the tepid water and stir until the yeast has dissolved and formed a creamy liquid. If using dried yeast, sprinkle it over half the tepid water and leave in a warm place for 10 minutes until frothy.
Sift the flour and salt either on to a clean working surface or into a large mixing bowl. Make a well in the centre of the dry ingredients and add the yeast liquid together with the remaining tepid water. Mix the dry ingredients into the liquid and work into a ball.
Knead the dough on a floured working surface until it is smooth and elastic – this can be done in an electric mixer fitted with a dough hook, or in a food processor. Form the dough into a ball and put into a lightly floured bowl, covered with a damp cloth. Leave in a warm place until the dough has doubled in size – about 1–1½ hours.
Serves 4–6

Pizza alla napoletana
Neapolitan tomato pizza

Metric	Imperial
Basic Pizza Dough (see left)	Basic Pizza Dough (see left)
olive oil	olive oil
450 g tomatoes, skinned and roughly chopped	1 lb tomatoes, skinned and roughly chopped
1 garlic clove, peeled and crushed	1 garlic clove, peeled and crushed
salt	salt
freshly ground black pepper	freshly ground black pepper
225 g Mozzarella cheese, thinly sliced	8 oz Mozzarella cheese, thinly sliced
6 anchovy fillets, split lengthways	6 anchovy fillets, split lengthways
1 × 15 ml spoon chopped fresh basil or oregano	1 tablespoon chopped fresh basil or oregano

Preparation time: 15 minutes
Cooking time: 25 minutes
Oven: 230°C, 450°F, Gas Mark 8;
    190°C, 375°F, Gas Mark 5

This is the 'classic' amongst pizzas. Tomatoes and fresh herbs give this pizza its characteristic flavour (on no account be tempted to use canned tomatoes.) If you find it difficult to buy fresh basil or oregano, then look for the small jars of herbs that are preserved in oil. As a very last resort, use 1 × 5 ml spoon/1 teaspoon dried basil or oregano softened in 1 × 5 ml spoon/1 teaspoon boiling water.

Roll out the pizza dough into a circle about 1 cm/½ inch thick on a floured working surface. Place the circle of dough on to a greased baking sheet and press out to a circle 30–35 cm/12–14 inches in diameter, and no more than 5 mm/¼ inch thick. Pinch up the edges of the dough all round. Brush the surface of the pizza dough with olive oil.
Mix the chopped tomatoes with the garlic and salt and pepper to taste, and spread evenly over the pizza dough. Top with the slices of cheese and the anchovy fillets, and sprinkle with the herbs. Sprinkle olive oil generously over the pizza topping. Place in a pre-heated oven and bake for 15 minutes. Reduce the oven temperature and continue to bake for a further 10 minutes. Serve immediately, cut into wedges.
Serves 4–6

Variation:
Pizza alla Siciliana: omit the Mozzarella cheese. Add 75 g/3 oz stoned black olives, roughly chopped, to the above pizza topping.

Pizza; Pizza alla napoletana

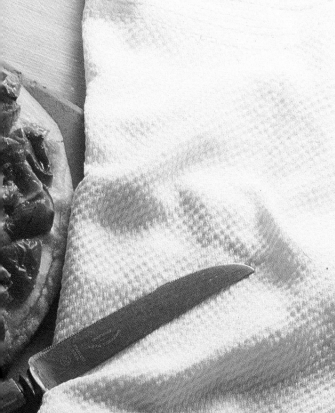

Pizza rustica
Cheese, salami and egg pie

Preparation time: 30 minutes
Cooking time: 30–35 minutes
Oven: 200°C, 400°F, Gas Mark 6

Metric
olive oil
2 medium onions, peeled
   and thinly sliced
1 garlic clove, peeled and
   crushed
275 g Ricotta cheese or
   sieved cottage cheese
3 hard-boiled eggs, chopped
100 g salami, chopped
salt
freshly ground black pepper
50 g stoned black olives,
   chopped
350 g puff pastry
2 × 15 ml spoons grated
   Parmesan cheese

Imperial
olive oil
2 medium onions, peeled
   and thinly sliced
1 garlic clove, peeled and
   crushed
10 oz Ricotta cheese or
   sieved cottage cheese
3 hard-boiled eggs, chopped
4 oz salami, chopped
salt
freshly ground black pepper
2 oz stoned black olives,
   chopped
12 oz puff pastry
2 tablespoons grated
   Parmesan cheese

Heat 6 × 15 ml spoons/6 tablespoons olive oil in a pan and gently fry the onions for 5 minutes. Allow to cool. Mix the onions with the garlic, Ricotta cheese, hard-boiled eggs, salami, salt and pepper to taste, and the chopped olives.

Divide the pastry into 2 equal portions. Roll out each one to a circle 25 cm/10 inches in diameter. Line a 23 cm/9 inch loose-bottomed flan tin with one circle of pastry. Press up the edges, and moisten with a little water or brush with beaten egg. Spread the Ricotta filling over the pastry. Lay the second pastry circle over the top and pinch the edges together to seal. Score the top surface of the pastry with the point of a sharp knife. Brush with oil and sprinkle with the grated Parmesan cheese. Place in a preheated oven and bake for 30–35 minutes until a rich golden brown. Serve hot, cut into wedges.
Serves 6

Torta di pomodori
Tomato tart

Metric	Imperial
4 × 15 ml spoons olive oil	4 tablespoons olive oil
750 g tomatoes, skinned, seeded and chopped	1½ lb tomatoes, skinned, seeded and chopped
1 garlic clove, peeled and crushed	1 garlic clove, peeled and crushed
salt	salt
freshly ground black pepper	freshly ground black pepper
3 × 15 ml spoons tomato purée	3 tablespoons tomato purée
grated rind of ½ orange	grated rind of ½ orange
1 × 15 ml spoon chopped fresh mint	1 tablespoon chopped fresh mint
generous pinch of sugar	generous pinch of sugar
225 g shortcrust pastry	8 oz shortcrust pastry
100 g Fontina cheese or other soft Italian cheese, cut into small cubes	4 oz Fontina cheese or other soft Italian cheese, cut into small cubes

Preparation time: 10 minutes
Cooking time: 55 minutes
Oven: 190°C, 375°F, Gas Mark 5

This tart has a better flavour if the pastry is made with butter. The Italians sometimes use a yeast pastry as a base for this tart, rather similar to a pizza dough.

Heat the oil in a large shallow pan and gently cook the tomatoes, stirring, for 3 minutes. Add the garlic, salt and pepper to taste, tomato purée and the orange rind. Simmer gently until the tomato mixture is pulpy and thick – stir from time to time to make sure that the tomato does not stick to the bottom of the pan and burn. Remove the tomato mixture from the heat, stir in the mint and sugar, and leave on one side until cool. Meanwhile, roll out the pastry and use to line a 23 cm/ 9 inch loose-bottomed flan tin. Line with greaseproof paper and baking beans, place in a preheated oven and bake 'blind' for 8 minutes. Remove the paper and beans from the pastry case. Stir the cheese into the tomato mixture. Spoon into the pastry case. Bake in the oven for 30 minutes. Serve while still warm.
Serves 6

Torta pasqualina
Genoese Easter pie

Metric	Imperial
750 g spinach, washed	1½ lb spinach, washed
salt	salt
freshly ground black pepper	freshly ground black pepper
generous pinch of grated nutmeg	generous pinch of grated nutmeg
2 eggs, lightly beaten	2 eggs, lightly beaten
50 g grated Parmesan cheese	2 oz grated Parmesan cheese
350 g puff pastry	12 oz puff pastry
8 canned artichoke hearts	8 canned artichoke hearts
100 g Italian blue cheese such as Dolcelatte, cut into small cubes	4 oz Italian blue cheese such as Dolcelatte, cut into small cubes
beaten egg, to glaze	beaten egg, to glaze

To garnish:	To garnish:
1 × 15 ml spoon pine kernels	1 tablespoon pine kernels
1 × 15 ml spoon chopped fresh mint	1 tablespoon chopped fresh mint

Preparation time: 30 minutes
Cooking time: 30–35 minutes
Oven: 200°C, 400°F, Gas Mark 6

Puff or flaky pastry can be used in this recipe, as both give equally good finished results. The great advantage with puff pastry is that you can buy it ready-made, either frozen or chilled.

Put the spinach in a pan and cook, without any water except that which clings to the leaves, for about 8 minutes until tender. Drain the spinach thoroughly and squeeze it well to remove as much moisture as possible. Season the spinach well with salt, pepper and nutmeg, and stir in the beaten eggs and grated Parmesan cheese.
Divide the pastry into 2 equal portions. Roll out each one to a circle 25 cm/10 inches in diameter. Line a 23 cm/9 inch loose-bottomed flan tin with one circle of pastry. Press up the edges well. Spread half the spinach mixture over the pastry. Top with the artichoke hearts and cheese. Spread over the remaining spinach mixture. Brush the pastry edges with beaten egg and top with the second circle of pastry. Pinch the edges together to seal. Glaze the top of the pie with beaten egg. Place in a preheated oven and bake for 30–35 minutes until golden brown. This unusual pie is equally delicious served hot or cold. Sprinkle with the pine kernels and mint before serving.
Serves 6

From the back, clockwise: Torta pasqualina;
Torta di pomodori; Pizza rustica

Pizza alla calabrese
Calabrian fish pizza

Metric	Imperial
Basic Pizza Dough (page 35)	Basic Pizza Dough (page 35)
olive oil	olive oil
1 medium onion, peeled and finely chopped	1 medium onion, peeled and finely chopped
750 g tomatoes, skinned, seeded and chopped	1½ lb tomatoes, skinned, seeded and chopped
2 garlic cloves, peeled and crushed	2 garlic cloves, peeled and crushed
salt	salt
freshly ground black pepper	freshly ground black pepper
1 × 200 g can tuna fish	1 × 7 oz can tuna fish
6 anchovy fillets, chopped	6 anchovy fillets, chopped
1 × 15 ml spoon capers	1 tablespoon capers
50 g stoned black olives, roughly chopped	2 oz stoned black olives, roughly chopped

Preparation time: 15 minutes
Cooking time: 35 minutes
Oven: 230°C, 450°F, Gas Mark 8;
190°C, 375°F, Gas Mark 5

Shape the basic pizza dough as in Pizza alla Napoletana. Heat 4 × 15 ml spoons/4 tablespoons olive oil in a pan and gently fry the onion for 2–3 minutes. Add the tomatoes, garlic and salt and pepper to taste. Cover and cook gently for 5 minutes. Add the tuna fish (undrained), chopped anchovies, capers and chopped black olives.
Brush the surface of the pizza dough with oil and spread the fish topping evenly over the top. Sprinkle olive oil generously over the pizza topping. Place in a preheated oven and bake for 15 minutes. Reduce the oven temperature and continue to bake for a further 10 minutes. Serve immediately, cut into wedges.
Serves 4–6

Calzoni alla napoletana
Pizza turnovers

Metric	Imperial
half quantity Basic Pizza Dough (page 35)	half quantity Basic Pizza Dough (page 35)
olive oil	olive oil
4 tomatoes, skinned, seeded and chopped	4 tomatoes, skinned, seeded and chopped
6 small slices Mozzarella cheese	6 small slices Mozzarella cheese
6 anchovy fillets	6 anchovy fillets
salt	salt
freshly ground black pepper	freshly ground black pepper
oil for deep frying	oil for deep frying

Preparation time: 20 minutes, plus proving
Cooking time: 5–6 minutes

Divide the pizza dough into 6 equal portions. Roll out each one to a very thin circle, approximately 13 cm/5 inches in diameter. Brush the centre of each circle with olive oil and the edges with water. Place a little chopped tomato, a slice of Mozzarella and an anchovy fillet to one side of each circle. Add salt and pepper to taste. Fold the other half of each pizza circle over the filling. Pinch the edges together to seal, forming half moon shapes.
Place the shaped turnovers on a floured baking sheet. Cover with a clean cloth and leave in a warm place to prove for 30 minutes. Deep fry the Calzoni in hot oil for 5–6 minutes until crisp and golden. Drain well and serve hot.
Serves 6

Pizza quattro stagioni
Four seasons pizza

Metric
Basic Pizza Dough
    (page 35)
olive oil
50 g button mushrooms,
    sliced
50 g Parma ham, cut into
    strips
6 stoned black olives, thinly
    sliced
4 canned artichoke hearts,
    thinly sliced
50 g Mozzarella cheese,
    sliced
1 tomato, skinned and
    sliced
salt
freshly ground black pepper

Imperial
Basic Pizza Dough
    (page 35)
olive oil
2 oz button mushrooms,
    sliced
2 oz Parma ham, cut into
    strips
6 stoned black olives, thinly
    sliced
4 canned artichoke hearts,
    thinly sliced
2 oz Mozzarella cheese,
    sliced
1 tomato, skinned and
    sliced
salt
freshly ground black pepper

Preparation time: 20 minutes
Cooking time: 30 minutes
Oven: 230°C, 450°F, Gas Mark 8;
        190°C, 375°F, Gas Mark 5

Shape the basic pizza dough as in Pizza alla Napole-tana. Heat 3 × 15 ml spoons/3 tablespoons olive oil in a pan and gently fry the sliced mushrooms for 5 minutes. Brush the surface of the pizza dough with oil and mark gently into four equal sections. Place the fried mushrooms over one section of pizza; the ham and olives over a second section; the artichoke hearts over the third section; and the Mozzarella cheese and tomato over the fourth section.

Season the pizza topping with salt and pepper and sprinkle generously with olive oil. Place in a preheated oven and bake for 15 minutes. Reduce the oven temperature and continue to bake for a further 10 minutes. Serve immediately, cut into wedges.

Serves 4–6

Pizza alla calabrese; Calzoni alla napoletana;
Pizza quattro stagioni

SAUCES AND PRESERVES

Italians treat their sauces with the same respect that the French do. They produce some particularly delicious sauces to go with pasta, turning a simple spaghetti or fettucine into something rather special. Mostarda di Cremona is the classic Italian preserve.

Pesto alla genovese
Green herb sauce

Metric	Imperial
1 large bunch basil leaves	1 large bunch basil leaves
3 garlic cloves, peeled	3 garlic cloves, peeled
25 g pine kernels	1 oz pine kernels
salt	salt
freshly ground black pepper	freshly ground black pepper
150 ml olive oil	1/4 pint olive oil
little boiling water	little boiling water

Preparation time: 5 minutes

The Italians feel strongly that this sauce should be made with a pestle and mortar, but it is much quicker if you use a liquidizer, and it tastes just the same. The sauce is served with different varieties of pasta, and as a flavouring for many soups such as minestrone.

Put the basil leaves into the liquidizer together with the garlic, pine kernels, salt and pepper to taste, and the olive oil. Blend until smooth. Thin to the desired consistency with a little boiling water. Pesto keeps well in a screw-top jar in the refrigerator for up to 6 days.

Variation:
Pesto di Formaggio: add 50 g/2 oz finely grated Pecorino or Parmesan cheese.

Salsa di pomodoro crudo
Uncooked tomato sauce

Metric	Imperial
450 g tomatoes, skinned and roughly chopped	*1 lb tomatoes, skinned and roughly chopped*
1 small onion, peeled and chopped	*1 small onion, peeled and chopped*
1 garlic clove, peeled and crushed	*1 garlic clove, peeled and crushed*
1 × 15 ml spoon chopped fresh parsley	*1 tablespoon chopped fresh parsley*
1 × 15 ml spoon chopped fresh basil	*1 tablespoon chopped fresh basil*
generous pinch of caster sugar	*generous pinch of caster sugar*
200 ml olive oil	*1/3 pint olive oil*
salt	*salt*
freshly ground black pepper	*freshly ground black pepper*

Preparation time: 4–5 minutes

This uncooked tomato sauce is usually served cold, but can be heated through gently if preferred. Large ripe plum tomatoes ideally should be used.

Put the tomatoes, onion, garlic, herbs, sugar, olive oil and salt and pepper to taste into a liquidizer and blend until smooth. The consistency can be adjusted by adding a little extra oil or a little boiling water.
Can be stored in a covered container in the refrigerator for up to 3 days.

From the left: Pesto alla genovese;
Salsa di pomodoro crudo; Mostarda di cremona

Mostarda di cremona
Mustard syrup preserve

Metric	Imperial
thinly pared rind of 1 lemon	*thinly pared rind of 1 lemon*
thinly pared rind of 1 orange	*thinly pared rind of 1 orange*
25 g root ginger, bruised	*1 oz root ginger, bruised*
50 g mustard seeds	*2 oz mustard seeds*
white wine vinegar	*white wine vinegar*
1 kg granulated sugar	*2 lb granulated sugar*
1 kg pears, peeled, cored and quartered	*2 lb pears, peeled, cored and quartered*
450 g peaches, skinned, stoned and quartered	*1 lb peaches, skinned, stoned and quartered*
450 g apricots, skinned, stoned and halved	*1 lb apricots, skinned, stoned and halved*
12 maraschino cherries	*12 maraschino cherries*

Preparation time: 25 minutes
Cooking time: 45 minutes

Mostarda di Cremona is one of the most popular condiments in Italy, but it is hardly known in this country – it is a delicious fruit pickle, preserved in a semi-sweet mustard syrup. It makes a tasty accompaniment to Italian cured meats and slicing sausages, and San Daniele con Ricotta (page 14).

Tie the fruit rinds, root ginger and mustard seeds in a piece of muslin. Put the muslin bag into a saucepan with 600 ml/1 pint white wine vinegar. Bring to the boil and simmer gently for 30 minutes.
Remove the muslin bag and make up the liquid to 600 ml/1 pint with white wine vinegar. Add the sugar and stir over a gentle heat until dissolved. Simmer the syrup for 5 minutes. Add the prepared fruits to the syrup and simmer for a further 5 minutes.
Remove the fruits with a perforated spoon and pack into clean warm jars. Boil the syrup for 5 minutes, then strain it over the fruit and cool. Seal the jars. Store for 1 month before using. Keeps up to 1 year.

Salsa verde
Green sauce

Metric	Imperial
200 ml olive oil	⅓ pint olive oil
juice of 1 lemon	juice of 1 lemon
3 × 15 ml spoons finely chopped fresh parsley	3 tablespoons finely chopped fresh parsley
6 anchovy fillets, finely chopped	6 anchovy fillets, finely chopped
2 × 15 ml spoons capers	2 tablespoons capers
2 garlic cloves, peeled and crushed	2 garlic cloves, peeled and crushed
salt	salt
freshly ground black pepper	freshly ground black pepper

Preparation time: 3 minutes, plus standing

This sauce is the traditional accompaniment to Bollito Misto (mixed boiled meats). It is also good served with any simple pasta. A little freshly grated horseradish is sometimes added for a more pungent flavour.

Mix together the olive oil, lemon juice, parsley, anchovies, capers, garlic and salt and pepper to taste. Leave the sauce covered, at room temperature, for 4 hours before serving, to allow the flavours to mature. Not suitable for storage.

Agliata
Garlic and breadcrumb sauce

Metric	Imperial
2 garlic cloves, peeled and crushed	2 garlic cloves, peeled and crushed
4 × 15 ml spoons fine white breadcrumbs	4 tablespoons fine white breadcrumbs
1 × 15 ml spoon wine vinegar	1 tablespoon wine vinegar
olive oil (see below)	olive oil (see below)
salt	salt
freshly ground black pepper	freshly ground black pepper

Preparation time: 5–6 minutes

Agliata is usually served as an accompaniment to baked or fried fish. The amount of oil you add is a matter of personal preference.

Put the garlic, breadcrumbs and vinegar into a bowl. Add the oil gradually, beating it in with a wooden spoon, until the required consistency. Add salt and pepper to taste. This will keep in a screwtop jar in the refrigerator for 2–3 days.

Maionese verde
Green mayonnaise

Metric	Imperial
3 egg yolks	3 egg yolks
250 ml olive oil (the greener the better)	8 fl oz olive oil (the greener the better)
salt	salt
freshly ground black pepper	freshly ground black pepper
few drops of lemon juice	few drops of lemon juice
2 × 15 ml spoons chopped fresh parsley	2 tablespoons chopped fresh parsley
1 × 15 ml spoon chopped fresh basil	1 tablespoon chopped fresh basil
1 × 15 ml spoon ground pistachio nuts (optional)	1 tablespoon ground pistachio nuts (optional)

Preparation time: 5–8 minutes

The Italians like their mayonnaise-based sauces really thick – they should drop off a spoon rather than run. If the mayonnaise shows signs of curdling, place another egg yolk into a bowl and gradually whisk in the prepared, curdled sauce.

Put the egg yolks into a bowl and break them up. Whisk in the oil very slowly, in a fine trickle, until all the oil has been absorbed. Add salt and pepper to taste and stir in the lemon juice, parsley, basil and nuts. Keeps up to 24 hours in a covered container.

From the left: Maionese verde; Agliata; Salsa verde

Bagna cauda
Hot garlic and anchovy sauce

Metric	Imperial
100 g butter	*4 oz butter*
8 × 15 ml spoons olive oil	*8 tablespoons olive oil*
3 garlic cloves, peeled and finely chopped	*3 garlic cloves, peeled and finely chopped*
8 anchovy fillets, finely chopped	*8 anchovy fillets, finely chopped*
salt	*salt*
freshly ground black pepper	*freshly ground black pepper*

Preparation time: 3 minutes
Cooking time: 5–8 minutes

This sauce is an absolute must for garlic lovers, but it is not at all gentle on those with weak digestions! Bagna cauda is served in Italy at any time throughout the day and night, with crisp raw vegetables or small fried fish for dunking . . . and plenty of red wine.

Put the butter, olive oil, garlic, anchovies and salt and pepper to taste into a saucepan and simmer for 5–8 minutes, until the anchovies have almost dissolved. Serve piping hot.
Not suitable for storage.

Bagna cauda; Salsa di pomodoro; Ragù; Besciamella

Salsa di pomodoro
Fresh tomato sauce

Metric	Imperial
1 kg tomatoes, roughly chopped	*2¼ lb tomatoes, roughly chopped*
1 small onion, peeled and finely chopped	*1 small onion, peeled and finely chopped*
1 large carrot, peeled and chopped	*1 large carrot, peeled and chopped*
2 sticks celery, finely chopped	*2 sticks celery, finely chopped*
1 garlic clove, peeled and crushed	*1 garlic clove, peeled and crushed*
2 × 15 ml spoons chopped fresh parsley	*2 tablespoons chopped fresh parsley*
1 × 2.5 ml spoon caster sugar	*½ teaspoon caster sugar*
salt	*salt*
freshly ground black pepper	*freshly ground black pepper*

Preparation time: 5 minutes
Cooking time: 20–25 minutes

Try to choose large plum tomatoes for the best flavours.

Put the tomatoes, onion, carrot, celery, garlic, parsley, sugar and salt and pepper to taste into a saucepan and simmer gently until the tomatoes have softened and almost turned to a purée. Sieve the sauce. Reheat the tomato sauce to serve with fish, meat or cooked pasta. Can be stored in a covered container in the refrigerator for up to 3 days.

Variation:
Salsa di Pomodoro e Basilico: add 2 × 15 ml spoons/ 2 tablespoons chopped fresh basil to the sieved sauce.

Ragù
Bolognese sauce

Metric	Imperial
25 g butter	1 oz butter
100 g Parma ham, chopped	4 oz Parma ham, chopped
1 medium onion, peeled and finely chopped	1 medium onion, peeled and finely chopped
2 sticks celery, finely chopped	2 sticks celery, finely chopped
1 large carrot, peeled and finely chopped	1 large carrot, peeled and finely chopped
225 g minced beef	8 oz minced beef
175 g chicken livers, trimmed and chopped	6 oz chicken livers, trimmed and chopped
1 × 15 ml spoon tomato purée	1 tablespoon tomato purée
150 ml dry white wine	¼ pint dry white wine
150 ml Brodo di Manzo (page 9)	¼ pint Brodo di Manzo (page 9)
1 garlic clove, peeled and crushed	1 garlic clove, peeled and crushed
pinch of ground cinnamon	pinch of ground cinnamon
salt	salt
freshly ground black pepper	freshly ground black pepper

Preparation time: 5 minutes
Cooking time: 40 minutes

Ragù is the traditional meat sauce to serve with simple pasta dishes, and it is one of the best base sauces to use for lasagne. For a very smooth sauce, a little cream is sometimes added, and for a really thick strongly-flavoured sauce, it is simmered for a little longer.

Melt the butter in a pan and gently fry the chopped ham for 3 minutes. Add the onion, celery and carrot and cook in the fat until they are lightly browned. Add the minced beef to the vegetables and stir over the heat for 2 minutes. Add the livers, tomato purée, wine, Brodo di Manzo, garlic, cinnamon, salt and pepper. Cover and simmer gently for 30 minutes.
Not suitable for storage.

Besciamella
Savoury white sauce

Metric	Imperial
750 ml milk	1¼ pints milk
1 bay leaf	1 bay leaf
1 small onion, peeled and stuck with 3 cloves	1 small onion, peeled and stuck with 3 cloves
40 g butter	1½ oz butter
2 × 15 ml spoons plain flour, sifted	2 tablespoons plain flour, sifted
salt	salt
freshly ground black pepper	freshly ground black pepper
pinch of grated nutmeg	pinch of grated nutmeg

Preparation time: 5 minutes, plus infusing
Cooking time: 20 minutes

Put the milk into a pan with the bay leaf and onion. Bring the milk to the boil, remove from the heat and leave to infuse for about 30 minutes. Strain. Meanwhile melt the butter in another pan until bubbles start to form – do not allow the butter to colour. Add the flour and stir over the heat to a thick creamy paste. Gradually stir in the strained milk. Bring the sauce to the boil, stirring, and simmer gently for 10 minutes. Add salt, pepper and nutmeg to taste and use as required.
Not suitable for storage.

FISH

Italy is such a long thin country, with so many of its regions bordering on to the sea, it is hardly surprising that it is a country devoted to fish. Not only do the Italians have a wide variety of fish at their disposal, but they also excel at cooking it. Venice is the home of some of the best fish dishes – such as Filetti di Sogliola.

46

Branzino con agliata
Sea bass with lemon and thyme

Metric	Imperial
1 sea bass, weighing about 1.25 kg, scaled and cleaned	*1 sea bass, weighing about 2½–2¾ lb, scaled and cleaned*
salt	*salt*
freshly ground black pepper	*freshly ground black pepper*
1 lemon, thinly sliced	*1 lemon, thinly sliced*
3 small sprigs fresh thyme	*3 sprigs fresh thyme*
50 g butter	*2 oz butter*
3 × 15 ml spoons olive oil	*3 tablespoons olive oil*
1 garlic clove, peeled and crushed	*1 garlic clove, peeled and crushed*
1 yellow pepper, cored, seeded and cut into thin strips	*1 yellow pepper, cored, seeded and cut into thin strips*
Agliata (page 42)	*Agliata (page 42)*

Preparation time: 5 minutes
Cooking time: 35–40 minutes
Oven: 200°C, 400°F, Gas Mark 6

Season the sea bass inside and out with salt and pepper. Place the fish in a greased ovenproof dish, one that is large enough to take the whole fish without bending it. Put the lemon slices and thyme into the cavity of the fish. Heat the butter and olive oil in a pan and gently cook the garlic and strips of pepper for 3–4 minutes. Spoon over the fish. Place in a preheated oven and bake for 30–35 minutes. Serve with a bowl of Agliata.
Serves 4–6

Spiedini di scampi
Scampi and mozzarella kebabs

Metric	Imperial
16 large fresh or frozen scampi, thawed	*16 large fresh or frozen scampi, thawed*
350 g Mozzarella cheese, cut into 2 cm cubes	*12 oz Mozzarella cheese, cut into ¾ inch cubes*
salt	*salt*
freshly ground black pepper	*freshly ground black pepper*
plain flour	*plain flour*
2 eggs, beaten	*2 eggs, beaten*
6 × 15 ml spoons fine breadcrumbs	*6 tablespoons fine breadcrumbs*
oil for deep frying	*oil for deep frying*
grated rind and juice of 1 lemon	*grated rind and juice of 1 lemon*
3 bay leaves, finely crushed	*3 bay leaves, finely crushed*
Bagna Cauda (page 44)	*Bagna Cauda (page 44)*

Preparation time: 20 minutes, plus chilling
Cooking time: 4–5 minutes

Cut the heads and tails from the scampi and remove the outer shells. Thread the scampi lengthways with the cubes of cheese on to 4 kebab skewers. Season with salt and pepper, and dust with flour. Dip each kebab into the beaten egg and coat thoroughly with breadcrumbs. Chill for 1 hour.
Lower the prepared kebabs into a pan of hot oil and deep fry for 4–5 minutes until crisp and golden. Drain the kebabs on paper towels and put on to a heated serving dish. Sprinkle with lemon rind and juice and the bay leaves. Serve with Bagna Cauda sauce.

Branzino con agliata; Spiedini di scampi

Baccalà alla chioggiota
Creamed salt cod

Metric	Imperial
750 g salt cod	1½ lb salt cod
300 ml milk	½ pint milk
600 ml water	1 pint water
150 ml olive oil	¼ pint olive oil
2 garlic cloves, peeled and crushed	2 garlic cloves, peeled and crushed
salt	salt
freshly ground black pepper	freshly ground black pepper

Preparation time: 20 minutes, plus soaking
Cooking time: 1–1½ hours

Baccalà is quite rich in flavour and needs to be eaten with something that offsets the richness. As an alternative to serving it as a main course it can be served in small portions as a starter with crusty bread. It is equally good eaten cold.
Although salt cod is traditionally used in this fish dish, smoked cod fillet makes a much more readily available and perfectly acceptable alternative, for those who cannot buy the salted fish. Soak the smoked cod fillet in water for 4 hours. Poach gently in milk and then proceed as in the method given.

Soak the salt cod in water for 48 hours, changing the water at least 4 times during that time. Drain the salt cod and put into a saucepan with the milk and water. Bring to the boil and simmer gently for 1–1½ hours until tender and the flesh flakes easily with a fork. Drain the fish and discard all the skin and bone.
Flake the salt cod flesh and pound it with a pestle and mortar until smooth (this can be done in a food processor or liquidizer). Gradually beat in the olive oil, and add garlic, salt and pepper to taste – go carefully with the salt. Heat the mixture through in the top of a double saucepan or in a bowl over a pan of simmering water. Either serve with croûtons of bread and black olives, or with Polenta (page 32).
Serves 8 as a starter

Filetti di sogliola
Sweet sour sole fillets

Metric	Imperial
olive oil	olive oil
2 large onions, peeled and thinly sliced	2 large onions, peeled and thinly sliced
2 × 15 ml spoons lemon juice	2 tablespoons lemon juice
2 × 15 ml spoons dry white wine	2 tablespoons dry white wine
2 × 5 ml spoons caster sugar	2 teaspoons caster sugar
salt	salt
freshly ground black pepper	freshly ground black pepper
50 g raisins	2 oz raisins
50 g pine kernels	2 oz pine kernels
750 g baby sole fillets	1½ lb baby sole fillets
plain flour	plain flour

Preparation time: 5 minutes, plus chilling
Cooking time: 10 minutes

Although the fish is served cold in this recipe, the Venetians often serve it hot with Polenta (page 32). For a more economical dish, you can substitute small plaice fillets for the sole.

Heat 8 × 15 ml spoons/8 tablespoons olive oil in a large shallow pan and gently cook the sliced onion for 5 minutes until soft. Add the lemon juice, white wine, sugar and salt and pepper to taste. Bring to the boil and simmer for 2 minutes. Add the raisins and pine kernels.
Dust the sole fillets lightly with flour. Shallow fry the fish in olive oil for 1 minute on each side. Drain the sole fillets on paper towels and arrange slightly overlapping in a shallow serving dish with a rim. Spoon over the onion mixture. Cover the dish and chill overnight.

Baccalà alla chioggiota; Filetti di sogliola; Tinca carpionata

Tinca carpionata
Marinated mixed fish

Metric	*Imperial*
2 small red mullet, filleted	2 small red mullet, filleted
2 small trout, filleted	2 small trout, filleted
4 small sardines, cleaned	4 small sardines, cleaned
flour	flour
olive oil	olive oil
salt	salt
freshly ground black pepper	freshly ground black pepper
1 onion, peeled and thinly sliced	1 onion, peeled and thinly sliced
2 garlic cloves, peeled and crushed	2 garlic cloves, peeled and crushed
150 ml red wine	¼ pint red wine
1 large red pepper, cored, seeded and cut into thin shreds	1 large red pepper, cored, seeded and cut into thin shreds
1 × 15 ml spoon chopped fresh oregano	1 tablespoon chopped fresh oregano

Preparation time: 5 minutes, plus chilling
Cooking time: 8–10 minutes

Dust the filleted fish and the sardines lightly in flour. Heat about 4 × 15 ml spoons/4 tablespoons olive oil in a pan and shallow fry the fish for 1–2 minutes on each side. Drain the fish and place in a shallow serving dish with a rim. Add salt and pepper to taste. Heat 3 × 15 ml spoons/3 tablespoons olive oil and fry the onion and garlic for 5 minutes. Add the wine and red pepper, and boil briskly for 1 minute. Stir in a further 6 × 15 ml spoons/6 tablespoons olive oil and spoon over the fish. Sprinkle with the oregano. Cover and chill for 4 hours.

Cassola con verdure
Fish and vegetable stew

Metric	Imperial
1.5 kg mixed fish (see below)	3 lb mixed fish (see below)
4 × 15 ml spoons olive oil	4 tablespoons olive oil
2 onions, peeled and sliced	2 onions, peeled and sliced
2 garlic cloves, peeled and crushed	2 garlic cloves, peeled and crushed
2 × 15 ml spoons tomato purée	2 tablespoons tomato purée
750 g tomatoes, skinned, seeded and chopped	1½ lb tomatoes, skinned, seeded and chopped
300 ml red wine	½ pint red wine
generous pinch of chilli powder	generous pinch of chilli powder
salt	salt
freshly ground black pepper	freshly ground black pepper
4 courgettes, cut into thick rings	4 courgettes, cut into thick rings
1 medium aubergine, cut into large cubes	1 medium aubergine, cut into large cubes
4 slices crusty bread, toasted or fried	4 slices crusty bread, toasted or fried

Preparation time: 35–40 minutes
Cooking time: 1 hour 40 minutes

The greater the variety of fish used in this casserole, the better the flavour and finished appearance. Choose three or more from the following – mullet, halibut steak or cutlet, skate, bream, squid, large prawns or mussels. Chilli powder is very hot and can vary in strength depending on the manufacturer, so it is wise to use it cautiously.

Cut off the heads and tails from the whole fish i.e. mullet and bream. Shell the prawns, removing the heads and tails. Clean the squid (page 10). Put the fish heads and tails and prawn shells into a pan with 1.25 litres/2¼ pints water. Bring to the boil and simmer for 30 minutes.
Cut the mullet, halibut, skate and bream into neat chunks about 5 cm/2 inches square, and the squid into rings. Scrub the mussels. Heat the oil in a pan and fry the onion for 5 minutes. Add the garlic, tomato purée, tomatoes, red wine, 900 ml/1½ pints of the strained fish stock, chilli powder and salt and pepper to taste. Simmer for 15 minutes. Add the squid, courgettes and aubergine and simmer gently for 30 minutes. Add the mullet, skate, bream and halibut and cook for a further 10 minutes. Finally, add the prawns and mussels and continue cooking for a further 10 minutes. (Discard any mussels that have not opened.) Put a slice of the bread into each serving bowl and ladle the stew on top.

Polpi in purgatorio
Octopus in a chilli sauce

Metric	Imperial
1 octopus, weighing about 1 kg, cleaned (see below)	1 octopus, weighing about 2¼ lb, cleaned (see below)
1 onion, peeled and sliced	1 onion, peeled and sliced
2 garlic cloves, peeled and chopped	2 garlic cloves, peeled and chopped
½ lemon	½ lemon
1 bay leaf	1 bay leaf
handful of parsley stalks	handful of parsley stalks
1 litre water	1¾ pints water
salt	salt
freshly ground black pepper	freshly ground black pepper
600 ml Salsa di Pomodoro (page 44)	1 pint Salsa di Pomodoro (page 44)
1 × 2.5 ml spoon chilli powder	½ teaspoon chilli powder
2 × 15 ml spoons chopped fresh parsley	2 tablespoons chopped fresh parsley

Preparation time: 15 minutes
Cooking time: 1 hour 40 minutes – 2 hours 10 minutes

The octopus that is available in this country has usually already been cleaned, and has received a ferocious bashing to make it tender. One chain of fishmongers in this country does sell octopus quite frequently, but if you find it difficult to buy, then use squid instead. Allow about the same amount of squid, prepare the squid (page 10), cut it into rings and boil for 45 minutes. Chilli powder is very hot and can vary in strength depending on the manufacturer, so it is wise to use it cautiously.

Put the octopus into a pan with the onion, garlic, lemon, bay leaf, parsley stalks, water and salt and pepper. Bring to the boil and simmer gently for 1½–2 hours until tender. Remove the octopus carefully from its cooking liquid and rinse under running water – discard the cooking liquid. Rub off the outer skin from the octopus and the scaley bosses (knobbly protrusions). Cut the octopus into even-sized pieces. Put the Salsa di Pomodoro into a pan and add the chilli powder, parsley and salt and pepper to taste. Add the chopped octopus and simmer gently for 10 minutes. Serve hot with plain boiled rice or Polenta (page 32). Serves 4–6

From the back: Cassola con verdure; Polpi in purgatorio

Triglie al cartoccio
Red mullet cooked with herbs

Metric	Imperial
4 medium red mullet, cleaned	4 medium red mullet, cleaned
salt	salt
freshly ground black pepper	freshly ground black pepper
olive oil	olive oil
2 garlic cloves, peeled and finely chopped	2 garlic cloves, peeled and finely chopped
1 × 15 ml spoon chopped fresh thyme	1 tablespoon chopped fresh thyme
1 × 15 ml spoon chopped fresh rosemary	1 tablespoon chopped fresh rosemary
150 ml red wine	¼ pint red wine

Preparation time: 25 minutes
Cooking time: 35–40 minutes
Oven: 190°C, 375°F, Gas Mark 5

If you wished to be really authentic, you would make the 'cooking bags' from oiled greaseproof paper, but this is exceedingly tricky – it is much easier to wrap each fish in a parcel of foil.

Season each mullet inside and out with salt and pepper. Cut 8 rectangles of foil, double the width of each fish and half as long again as the fish. Brush the shiny side of 4 pieces of the foil with oil. Place on a large baking sheet, oiled side uppermost, and place a mullet along the centre of each one. Pull up the edges of the foil around each fish to form a rim. Put 1 × 15 ml spoon/1 tablespoon oil over each fish, a sprinkling of garlic, thyme and rosemary, and 2 × 15 ml spoons/2 tablespoons red wine.
Oil the shiny side of the remaining pieces of foil, and place oiled side down over each fish. Pinch the foil seams together to seal the whole way round each 'parcel', completely enclosing the fish. Place in a preheated oven and bake for 35–40 minutes. Cut a hole in the top of each parcel just before serving, to allow the excess steam to escape.

Triglie al cartoccio; Sarde alla cetrarese; Fritto misto mare

Sarde alla cetrarese
Baked sardines with fennel

Metric	Imperial
2 medium heads of fennel	2 medium heads of fennel
50 g butter	2 oz butter
olive oil	olive oil
1 garlic clove, peeled and crushed	1 garlic clove, peeled and crushed
1 × 15 ml spoons chopped fresh oregano	1 tablespoon chopped fresh oregano
12 fairly large fresh sardines	12 fairly large fresh sardines
juice of ½ lemon	juice of ½ lemon
salt	salt
freshly ground black pepper	freshly ground black pepper

Preparation time: 20 minutes
Cooking time: 25–26 minutes
Oven: 190°C, 375°F, Gas Mark 5

Remove the feathery tops from the fennel, if any, and reserve for garnish. Cut a thin slice from the base of each bulb of fennel and remove any discoloured patches with a potato peeler. Cut each bulb of fennel in half and shred finely.
Heat the butter in a large shallow pan with 4 × 15 ml spoons/4 tablespoons olive oil and gently cook the fennel and garlic for 5–6 minutes until the fennel starts to soften. Put the fennel into the base of a shallow greased ovenproof dish. Sprinkle with half the oregano. Brush the sardines with olive oil and lay them on top of the fennel. Sprinkle with the remaining oregano, lemon juice and salt and pepper. Place in a preheated oven and bake for 20 minutes. Garnish with the fennel tops.

Fritto misto mare
Mixed fried fish

Metric
100 g plain flour
salt
1 × 15 ml spoon olive oil
200 ml tepid water
2 egg whites
4 small whole sardines,
  cleaned
2 sole fillets, cut into finger-
  width strips
4 small shelled scallops
12 unshelled prawns
8 shelled mussels (bottled in
  brine)
about 16 whitebait
oil for deep frying
freshly ground black pepper

To garnish:
parsley
lemon wedges

Imperial
4 oz plain flour
salt
1 tablespoon olive oil
⅓ pint tepid water
2 egg whites
4 small whole sardines,
  cleaned
2 sole fillets, cut into finger-
  width strips
4 small shelled scallops
12 unshelled prawns
8 shelled mussels (bottled in
  brine)
about 16 whitebait
oil for deep frying
freshly ground black pepper

To garnish:
parsley
lemon wedges

Preparation time: 20 minutes, plus standing
Cooking time: 5–6 minutes

Fritto Misto Mare is served in most restaurants along the Italian coast – the fish that is included depends very much on what is locally available. If you wish to use fresh mussels, steam them for 2–3 minutes until the shells open. Twist the shells in opposite directions until they separate and, using the empty half shell as a scoop, ease out the mussel from the remaining shell. If the fresh varieties of any of these fish are unavailable, then frozen ones can be used – make sure that they are thoroughly thawed and pat them dry on paper towels. If your fryer is not large enough, cook the fish in batches and keep warm in a low oven, uncovered.

To make the batter, sift the flour into a bowl with 1 × 5 ml/1 teaspoon salt. Add the olive oil and tepid water and whisk until smooth and creamy. Cover the bowl and leave at room temperature for 1 hour.
Whisk the egg whites until they hold in soft peaks. Fold lightly but thoroughly into the batter. Dip the sardines into the batter, allow the excess batter to drain off and then lower into the pan of hot oil – the sardines go in first as they take the longest to cook. Next, dip the sole strips and scallops into the batter and add to the hot oil. Dip the prawns and mussels into the batter and add to the oil. Finally, dip the whitebait into the batter and add to the oil. Cook the whitebait for about 45 seconds, by which time all the other fish will be cooked. Drain thoroughly on paper towels. Season with salt and pepper and serve immediately garnished with parsley and lemon.

MEAT, POULTRY AND GAME

Italians have never been great meat eaters. This may be due to the climate, to the history of the country, or just the fact that they actually prefer to eat other foods. When Italians do cook meat, however, they tend to do it well and the meat is usually of particularly good quality, especially the veal. Much of the pork consumed in Italy is eaten in the form of sausages, rarely eaten as a roast joint as we know it. Turkey is very popular, and it is treated as a special dish in many parts of the country at Christmas, especially in Milan.

Ossobuco
Veal, tomato and wine stew

Metric	Imperial
4 thick pieces shin of veal	4 thick pieces shin of veal
salt	salt
freshly ground black pepper	freshly ground black pepper
plain flour	plain flour
50 g butter	2 oz butter
2 × 15 ml spoons oil	2 tablespoons oil
300 ml dry white wine	½ pint dry white wine
2 garlic cloves, peeled and crushed	2 garlic cloves, peeled and crushed
450 g tomatoes, skinned, seeded and chopped	1 lb tomatoes, skinned, seeded and chopped

To garnish:

1 garlic clove, peeled and finely chopped	1 garlic clove, peeled and finely chopped
grated rind of 1 lemon	grated rind of 1 lemon
2 × 15 ml spoons chopped fresh parsley	2 tablespons chopped fresh parsley

Preparation time: 10 minutes
Cooking time: 1 hour 10 minutes

Select your pieces of veal carefully, choosing those that have a generous amount of marrow in the shin bone – it is highly nutritious and has a delicious flavour. The Italians remove the marrow with a specially shaped fork (rather like a lobster pick) and eat it spread thickly on bread. Make sure that the pieces of veal remain upright during cooking, otherwise the marrow will be lost in the sauce.

Sprinkle the pieces of veal with salt and pepper and dust them with flour. Heat the butter and oil in a large shallow pan and brown the pieces of veal on both sides, then turn each piece of veal so that it is standing upright. Add the wine, garlic and tomatoes and bring to the boil. Cover and simmer gently for 1 hour – the meat should almost be falling off the bones.
For the garnish, which the Italians call 'gremolata', mix the chopped garlic with the grated lemon rind and parsley. Sprinkle over the cooked Ossobuco. Serve with Risotto alla Milanese (page 30).

Ossobuco; Farsumagru

Farsumagru
Stuffed spiced breast of veal

Metric	Imperial
1 × 1.5 kg piece boned breast of veal	1 × 3½ lb piece boned breast of veal
salt	salt
freshly ground black pepper	freshly ground black pepper

Stuffing:

450 g minced pork	1 lb minced pork
1 × 100 g piece Parma ham, chopped	1 × 4 oz piece Parma ham, chopped
2 × 15 ml spoons chopped fresh parsley	2 tablespoons chopped fresh parsley
1 × 2.5 ml spoon ground coriander	½ teaspoon ground coriander
1 × 2.5 ml spoon mixed spice	½ teaspoon mixed spice
50 g grated Parmesan cheese	2 oz grated Parmesan cheese
1 large garlic clove, peeled and crushed	1 large garlic clove, peeled and crushed

Sauce:

750 g tomatoes, skinned, seeded and chopped	1½ lb tomatoes, skinned, seeded and chopped
600 ml Brodo di Pollo (page 8)	1 pint Brodo di Pollo (page 8)
1 garlic clove, peeled and crushed	1 garlic clove, peeled and crushed
1 × 15 ml spoon chopped fresh basil	1 tablespoon chopped fresh basil
1 × 150 g can tomato purée	1 × 5 oz can tomato purée
salt	salt
freshly ground black pepper	freshly ground black pepper

Preparation time: 25 minutes
Cooking time: 2 hours 5 minutes

This dish goes under many different names in Italy, depending on the region from which it originates.

Trim the breast of veal to a neat rectangular shape, with the boned surface uppermost. Season well with salt and pepper. Mix all the ingredients together for the stuffing. Spread the stuffing evenly over the veal. Roll up from one of the short sides into a sausage shape, like a Swiss roll. Do not roll too tightly. Tie into a neat shape with fine string.
To make the sauce, put all the ingredients into a pan, one that is large enough to take the rolled veal. Simmer the sauce for 5 minutes. Add the veal to the sauce in the pan. Cover and simmer gently for 2 hours. Serve cut in fairly thick slices, together with the sauce, accompanied by Risotto alla Milanese or Polenta (pages 30 and 32).

Scaloppine ghiottona
Veal with truffle and ham sauce

Metric	Imperial
4 very thin veal escalopes	4 very thin veal escalopes
plain flour	plain flour
6 × 15 ml spoons olive oil	6 tablespoons olive oil
175 g button mushrooms, sliced	6 oz button mushrooms, sliced
100 g Parma ham, cut into thin strips	4 oz Parma ham, cut into thin strips
1 × 5 ml spoon truffle paste (optional)	1 teaspoon truffle paste (optional)
1 garlic clove, peeled and crushed	1 garlic clove, peeled and crushed
salt	salt
freshly ground black pepper	freshly ground black pepper
225 g spaghetti	8 oz spaghetti
75 g butter	3 oz butter
2 × 15 ml spoons grated Parmesan cheese	2 tablespoons grated Parmesan cheese

Preparation time: 15 minutes
Cooking time: 15 minutes

Truffles are used quite extensively in Italian cooking, and they lend a characteristic flavour to many meat and pasta dishes. They are, however, very expensive to buy in this country, and until recently were only available in small cans. Some specialist food shops that stock a wide range of Italian produce now sell a truffle paste, which is reasonably priced. If you find it difficult to buy, it can be omitted from the recipe.

Cut each veal escalope into 4 or 5 pieces. Dust the pieces of veal in flour. Heat the olive oil in a pan and gently cook the mushrooms for 3 minutes. Stir in the ham, half the truffle paste, the garlic, and salt and pepper to taste.
Cook the spaghetti in a large pan of boiling salted water for 8–10 minutes until 'al dente'.
Meanwhile, melt the butter in a large shallow pan and cook the pieces of veal for about 1 minute on each side, stirring in the remaining truffle paste, and salt and pepper to taste.
Drain the spaghetti well and toss together with the hot mushroom and ham sauce. Spoon the spaghetti on to a heated serving dish and top with the pieces of cooked veal. Sprinkle with the Parmesan cheese and serve immediately.

Costolette alla milanese
Veal cutlet on the bone

Metric	Imperial
4 veal cutlets (thin chops), on the bone	4 veal cutlets (thin chops), on the bone
200 ml milk	1/3 pint milk
1 egg, beaten	1 egg, beaten
about 6 × 15 ml spoons fine breadcrumbs	about 6 tablespoons fine breadcrumbs
100 g butter	4 oz butter
2 × 15 ml spoons olive oil	2 tablespoons olive oil
salt	salt
freshly ground black pepper	freshly ground black pepper
To garnish:	**To garnish:**
1 lemon, quartered	1 lemon, quartered
2 × 15 ml spoons chopped fresh parsley	2 tablespoons chopped fresh parsley

Preparation time: 20 minutes, plus chilling
Cooking time: 8 minutes

The veal cutlets are marinated in milk to soften and whiten the meat. Fry the cutlets immediately they have been coated in crumbs so that the outside becomes crisp and golden.

Holding each cutlet by the bone, batten the meat with a meat mallet or rolling pin to flatten it – do not make it too thin. Put the cutlets into a large shallow dish and pour over the milk. Cover the dish and chill for at least 1 hour.
Remove the cutlets from the milk and pat dry. Dip first into the beaten egg and then into the fine crumbs to give an even coating. Heat the butter and oil in a large shallow frying pan and cook the cutlets, seasoning them with salt and pepper, for 3–4 minutes on each side until crisp, golden and tender. Arrange the cooked cutlets on a heated serving dish and garnish with the lemon quarters dipped into the fresh parsley.

From the back: Scaloppine ghiottona;
Costolette di agnello; Costolette alla milanese

Costolette di agnello
Lamb cutlets with peppers

Preparation time: 10 minutes
Cooking time: 30 minutes

Yellow peppers add an appetizing colour to this dish, but you can use red peppers or all green ones.

Metric
8 lamb cutlets, trimmed
plain flour
6 × 15 ml spoons olive oil
2 medium yellow peppers,
    cored, seeded and sliced
2 medium green peppers,
    cored, seeded and sliced
2 garlic cloves, peeled and
    crushed
1 × 15 ml spoon chopped
    fresh oregano
2 × 15 ml spoons chopped
    fresh parsley
salt
freshly ground black pepper

Imperial
8 lamb cutlets, trimmed
plain flour
6 tablespoons olive oil
2 medium yellow peppers,
    cored, seeded and sliced
2 medium green peppers,
    cored, seeded and sliced
2 garlic cloves, peeled and
    crushed
1 tablespoon chopped fresh
    oregano
2 tablespoons chopped fresh
    parsley
salt
freshly ground black pepper

Dust the lamb cutlets in flour. Heat half the oil in a large shallow pan and cook the cutlets for 2–3 minutes on each side until golden. Remove the cutlets to a heated plate and keep warm.
Add the remaining oil to the pan, together with the peppers. Cook for 4–5 minutes until the peppers start to soften. Add the garlic, herbs, and salt and pepper to taste. Arrange the lamb cutlets on top. Cover the pan and cook gently for a further 15 minutes.

Polpette al pomodoro
Fried meatballs with cheese

Metric	Imperial
75 g 2-day old bread, crumbled	*3 oz 2-day old bread, crumbled*
6 × 15 ml spoons white wine	*6 tablespoons white wine*
500 g lean raw beef, finely minced	*1¼ lb lean raw beef, finely minced*
3 × 15 ml spoons chopped fresh parsley	*3 tablespoons chopped fresh parsley*
50 g grated Parmesan cheese	*2 oz grated Parmesan cheese*
salt	*salt*
freshly ground black pepper	*freshly ground black pepper*
2 egg yolks	*2 egg yolks*
plain flour	*plain flour*
175 g Mozzarella cheese, cut into small cubes	*6 oz Mozzarella cheese, cut into small cubes*
oil for shallow frying	*oil for shallow frying*
Salsa di Pomodoro e Basilico (page 44)	*Salsa di Pomodoro e Basilico (page 44)*

Preparation time: 20 minutes, plus standing
Cooking time: 12 minutes

Other minced lean meats can be used in place of beef – veal, pork, boned chicken, etc. If you find the moulding of the meatballs rather tricky, then the Mozzarella cheese can be omitted.

Mix the crumbled bread with the white wine and leave to stand for 15 minutes. Mix together with the minced beef, parsley, Parmesan cheese, salt and pepper to taste, and the egg yolks. Divide the mixture into small even-sized portions, about the size of a plum. Using floured hands, mould each one around a piece of cheese, so that the cheese is completely enclosed. Shallow fry the meatballs in hot oil for 6 minutes, turning them during cooking.
Heat the sauce in a separate pan. Add the drained meatballs and continue cooking over a moderate heat for 5 minutes. Serve with noodles or rice.

Fegato e animelle
Liver and sweetbreads with sage

Metric	Imperial
225 g calves' sweetbreads	*8 oz calves' sweetbreads*
salt	*salt*
350 g calves' liver, thinly sliced	*12 oz calves' liver, thinly sliced*
plain flour	*plain flour*
100 g butter	*4 oz butter*
2 × 15 ml spoons chopped fresh sage	*2 tablespoons chopped fresh sage*
juice of ½ lemon	*juice of ½ lemon*
freshly ground black pepper	*freshly ground black pepper*

Preparation time: 15 minutes, plus soaking
Cooking time: 12 minutes

Soak the sweetbreads in cold water for 2 hours, changing the water several times. Drain the sweetbreads and put them into a pan with sufficient fresh water to cover. Add a generous pinch of salt and simmer for 6 minutes. Plunge the sweetbreads into a bowl of cold water to firm up their texture. Trim off all the membrane and tiny tubes. Cut the sweetbreads into 1 cm/½ inch thick slices (you may find this easier if you chill the sweetbreads before slicing).
Dust the sweetbreads and liver in flour. Heat the butter and sage in a large shallow pan and cook the sweetbreads and liver over a moderate heat for 5 minutes, turning them from time to time. Add the lemon juice and pepper, and serve immediately.

Polpette al pomodoro; Fegato e animelle; Fegatini di pollo

58

Fegatini di pollo
Chicken livers in marsala sauce

Preparation time: 10–15 minutes
Cooking time: 30 minutes

Metric
firm Polenta, made with
    175 g polenta flour and
    about 600 ml water
    (page 32)
olive oil
1 onion, peeled and finely
    chopped
450 g chicken livers,
    roughly chopped
2 × 15 ml spoons plain flour
300 ml Brodo di Pollo
    (page 8)
4 × 15 ml spoons Marsala
100 g button mushrooms,
    sliced
1 × 2.5 ml spoon truffle
    paste
75 g Parma ham, chopped
salt
freshly ground black pepper
1 garlic clove, peeled and
    crushed
2 × 15 ml spoons coarsely
    chopped fresh parsley

Imperial
firm Polenta, made with
    6 oz polenta flour and
    about 1 pint water
    (page 32)
olive oil
1 onion, peeled and finely
    chopped
1 lb chicken livers, roughly
    chopped
2 tablespoons plain flour
½ pint Brodo di Pollo
    (page 8)
4 tablespoons Marsala
4 oz button mushrooms,
    sliced
½ teaspoon truffle
    paste
3 oz Parma ham, chopped
salt
freshly ground black pepper
1 garlic clove, peeled and
    crushed
2 tablespoons coarsely
    chopped fresh parsley

Put the cooked Polenta on to a floured working surface and roll out to a thickness of 1 cm/½ inch. Using a saucer as a guide, cut 4 circles from the Polenta dough. Heat 3 × 15 ml spoons/3 tablespoons olive oil and gently fry the onion for 4 minutes. Dust the chicken livers in the flour. Add the chicken livers to the pan and fry gently until sealed. Add the Brodo di Pollo, Marsala, mushrooms, truffle paste, ham, salt and pepper to taste, and the garlic. Simmer gently for 10–15 minutes until the mushrooms and livers are tender. Meanwhile, shallow fry the circles of Polenta dough in olive oil for 3–4 minutes on each side. Drain the fried Polenta and arrange on a heated serving dish. Spoon the chicken livers and their sauce over the Polenta. Sprinkle with chopped parsley.

Lepre in agrodolce
Hare in sweet sour sauce

Metric	Imperial
1 hare, prepared and cut into 6 serving pieces	1 hare, prepared and cut into 6 serving pieces
150 ml red wine vinegar	¼ pint red wine vinegar
4 × 15 ml spoons olive oil	4 tablespoons olive oil
salt	salt
freshly ground black pepper	freshly ground black pepper
1 × 15 ml spoon chopped fresh thyme	1 tablespoon chopped fresh thyme
50 g butter	2 oz butter
1 onion, peeled and thinly sliced	1 onion, peeled and thinly sliced
100 g Parma ham, chopped	4 oz Parma ham, chopped
plain flour	plain flour
300 ml red wine	½ pint red wine
300 ml Brodo di Manzo (page 9)	½ pint Brodo di Manzo (page 9)
1 × 2.5 ml spoon ground cinnamon	½ teaspoon ground cinnamon
50 g sultanas	2 oz sultanas
1 × 15 ml spoon chopped fresh mint	1 tablespoon chopped fresh mint
50 g granulated sugar	2 oz granulated sugar
2 × 15 ml spoons water	2 tablespoons water
4 × 15 ml spoons Marsala or sweet sherry	4 tablespoons Marsala or sweet sherry
50 g plain chocolate, grated	2 oz plain chocolate, grated

Preparation time: 20 minutes, plus chilling
Cooking time: about 2 hours

Put the pieces of hare into a shallow dish. Add half the red wine vinegar, the oil, salt and pepper to taste, and the chopped thyme. Cover and chill in the refrigerator for 4 hours. Remove the pieces of hare and pat dry on paper towels.
Melt the butter in a large pan and gently fry the onion and ham for 3 minutes. Dust the pieces of hare in flour and add to the hot fat. Cook until the hare is lightly browned on all sides. Gradually stir in the red wine and Brodo di Manzo. Add the cinnamon, sultanas, chopped mint, and salt and pepper to taste. Bring to the boil, cover and simmer for 1½ hours. Remove the pieces of hare to a heated serving dish and keep warm. Put the sugar and water into a small pan and stir until the sugar has dissolved. Boil to a lightly golden caramel. Immediately stir in the remaining red wine vinegar and the Marsala to prevent the sugar syrup from solidifying. Add to the cooking liquid from the hare, together with the grated chocolate.
Heat the sauce through and pour over the hare. Serve immediately with cooked red cabbage and a potato or simple pasta dish.
Serves 6

Stracotto di bue
Oxtail and red wine stew

Metric	Imperial
1.5 kg oxtail, cut into serving pieces	3 lb oxtail, cut into serving pieces
milk	milk
4 × 15 ml spoons olive oil	4 tablespoons olive oil
1 large onion, peeled and sliced	1 large onion, peeled and sliced
600 ml Barolo or other full-bodied red wine	1 pint Barolo or other full-bodied red wine
about 450 ml Brodo di Manzo (page 9)	about ¾ pint Brodo di Manzo (page 9)
bouquet garni	bouquet garni
1 garlic clove, peeled and crushed	1 garlic clove, peeled and crushed
3 sticks celery, chopped	3 sticks celery, chopped
6 tomatoes, skinned, seeded and chopped	6 tomatoes, skinned, seeded and chopped
4 large carrots, peeled and thinly sliced	4 large carrots, peeled and thinly sliced
2 bay leaves	2 bay leaves
75 g Parma ham, chopped	3 oz Parma ham, chopped
1 × 2.5 ml spoon ground cinnamon	½ teaspoon ground cinnamon
salt	salt
freshly ground black pepper	freshly ground black pepper

Preparation time: 15 minutes, plus chilling
Cooking time: 2 hours 40 minutes – 3 hours 10 minutes

Put the pieces of oxtail into a large shallow dish and add sufficient milk just to cover. Cover the dish and leave in a cool place for 2 hours. Discard the milk and drain the pieces of oxtail on paper towels.
Heat the oil in a large saucepan and fry the onion until lightly golden. Add the oxtail and gently fry until evenly browned on all sides. Add the wine, 450 ml/¾ pint Brodo di Manzo, bouquet garni and garlic. Bring to the boil, cover and simmer very gently for 1½ hours. Skim off any surface fat. If the liquid evaporates too quickly, then add extra Brodo di Manzo. Add the remaining ingredients and simmer gently for a further 1–1½ hours. In Italy the liquid is not usually thickened, but you may do so if preferred. Serve with crusty bread and follow with a simple salad.
Serves 4–6

Clockwise, from the back: Stracotto di bue;
Coniglio con olive; Lepre in agrodolce

Coniglio con olive
Rabbit in white wine with olives

Metric	Imperial
4 good-sized rabbit joints	*4 good-sized rabbit joints*
300 ml dry white wine	*½ pint dry white wine*
2 × 15 ml spoons chopped	*2 tablespoons chopped fresh*
* fresh sage*	* sage*
salt	*salt*
freshly ground black pepper	*freshly ground black pepper*
plain flour	*plain flour*
50 g butter	*2 oz butter*
2 × 15 ml spoons oil	*2 tablespoons oil*
1 large onion, peeled and	*1 large onion, peeled and*
* thinly sliced*	* thinly sliced*
300 ml Brodo di Pollo	*½ pint Brodo di Pollo*
* (page 8)*	* (page 8)*
12 large green olives	*12 large green olives*
3 × 15 ml spoons brandy	*3 tablespoons brandy*
12 whole blanched almonds	*12 whole blanched almonds*

Preparation time: 10–15 minutes, plus chilling
Cooking time: 1 hour

This rabbit dish is very good if prepared the night before, and then heated through prior to eating. Omit the almonds from the initial cooking, and add just before serving, otherwise they go very soft.

Prick the rabbit joints at regular intervals with a fine skewer. Put them into a shallow dish and add the wine, half the sage, and salt and pepper to taste. Chill for 4–6 hours. Drain the rabbit joints on paper towels and dust with flour. Reserve the marinade.
Heat the butter and oil in a large shallow pan and fry the onion for 3–4 minutes. Add the rabbit joints and cook until lightly browned. Stir in the marinade, Brodo di Pollo, remaining chopped sage and the olives. Cover the pan and cook gently for about 45 minutes until the rabbit is tender. Stir in the brandy and almonds and cook for a further 1–2 minutes. Serve hot with Risotto alla Milanese or Polenta (pages 30 and 32).

Pollo tonnato
Chicken in tuna fish sauce

Metric
4 chicken breasts, boned
    and skinned
1 medium onion, peeled
    and thinly sliced
1 bay leaf
strip of lemon peel
salt
freshly ground black pepper
300 ml dry white wine

Sauce:
2 egg yolks
juice of ½ lemon
300 ml olive oil
freshly ground black pepper
1 × 15 ml spoon capers
1 × 200 g can tuna fish
4 anchovy fillets

To garnish:
1 × 15 ml spoon capers
4 anchovy fillets, split in
    half lengthways
parsley sprigs

Imperial
4 chicken breasts, boned
    and skinned
1 medium onion, peeled
    and thinly sliced
1 bay leaf
strip of lemon peel
salt
freshly ground black pepper
½ pint dry white wine

Sauce:
2 egg yolks
juice of ½ lemon
½ pint olive oil
freshly ground black pepper
1 tablespoon capers
1 × 7 oz can tuna fish
4 anchovy fillets

To garnish:
1 tablespoon capers
4 anchovy fillets, split in
    half lengthways
parsley sprigs

Preparation time: 25 minutes, plus chilling
Cooking time: 20 minutes

This is a variation on the classic recipe, Vitello Tonnato, which uses a large piece of cooked veal – the veal is sliced while still hot and then masked with the strongly flavoured tuna sauce.

Put the chicken breasts into a shallow pan with the onion, bay leaf, lemon peel, salt and pepper to taste, and the wine. Cover and cook gently for about 20 minutes until the chicken is tender.
Meanwhile, to make the sauce: beat the egg yolks with the lemon juice. Gradually whisk in the oil, in a fine trickle, as if making a basic mayonnaise. Put the mayonnaise into the liquidizer, together with the capers, tuna fish, anchovy fillets and pepper to taste. Blend until smooth.
Put the drained chicken breasts on to a serving dish. Thin the tuna sauce to a coating consistency with a little of the chicken cooking liquid. Spoon the sauce over the chicken breasts while they are still warm. Chill for 4 hours, or overnight if preferred. Garnish with capers, anchovy fillets and parsley.

Pollo alla leccornia
Stuffed chicken

Metric
50 g butter
1 small onion, peeled and
    finely chopped
3 hard-boiled eggs, chopped
225 g chicken livers,
    chopped
100 g Pecorino cheese,
    crumbled
1 large stale roll, crumbled
750 ml dry white wine
freshly ground black pepper
1 garlic clove, peeled and
    crushed
1 × 2 kg chicken,
    prepared
sprig of fresh thyme
sprig of fresh tarragon
few fresh basil leaves
sprig of parsley

Imperial
2 oz butter
1 small onion, peeled and
    finely chopped
3 hard-boiled eggs, chopped
8 oz chicken livers,
    chopped
4 oz Pecorino cheese,
    crumbled
1 large stale roll, crumbled
1¾ pints dry white wine
freshly ground black pepper
1 garlic clove, peeled and
    crushed
1 × 4½ lb chicken,
    prepared
sprig of fresh thyme
sprig of fresh tarragon
few fresh basil leaves
sprig of parsley

Preparation time: 20 minutes
Cooking time: 1 hour 35 minutes–2 hours 5 minutes

Pecorino or Parmesan are the best cheeses to use for this tangy chicken stuffing. You should not find it necessary to add salt to the stuffing or to the chicken, due to the 'saltiness' of the cheese.

Melt the butter in a pan and gently fry the onion for 5 minutes. Mix the onion with the chopped hard-boiled eggs, chicken livers, cheese, crumbled bread roll, 6 × 15 ml spoons/6 tablespoons of the white wine, pepper and garlic. Push the stuffing firmly into the cavity of the chicken and truss with string.
Put the chicken into a large pan with the remaining wine and the herbs. Bring to the boil, cover and simmer gently for 1½–2 hours until the chicken is tender. Carve the chicken in the usual way, moistening each portion with a little of the cooking liquor. (It may be thickened, if preferred, with a little flour or cornflour). Accompany with fettuccine and a salad.
Serves 6

From the left: Pollo tonnato; Filetto al carpaccio; Pollo alla leccornia

Filetto al carpaccio
Raw steak with mustard sauce

Metric
2 egg yolks
juice of ½ lemon
300 ml olive oil
2 × 5 ml spoons French
  mustard
2 garlic cloves, peeled and
  crushed
salt
freshly ground black pepper
2 × 15 ml spoons capers
450 g best quality fillet
  steak
thin wedges of lemon, to
  garnish

Imperial
2 egg yolks
juice of ½ lemon
½ pint olive oil
2 teaspoons French
  mustard
2 garlic cloves, peeled and
  crushed
salt
freshly ground black pepper
2 tablespoons capers
1 lb best quality fillet
  steak
thin wedges of lemon, to
  garnish

Preparation time: 25 minutes

This is really Italy's answer to 'steak tartare' – in this recipe the meat is sliced paper thin, rather than being minced. It is important that the meat is very fresh and of a particularly high quality. The steak is easier to slice if chilled for 2–3 hours beforehand. Use a very sharp knife for cutting it, and only slice the steak immediately prior to eating, otherwise it will become dry and lose its characteristic colour.

To make the sauce, put the egg yolks into a bowl with the lemon juice. Beat with a whisk to break up the egg yolks. Gradually whisk in the olive oil, adding it in a fine trickle, until all the oil has been absorbed (as if making mayonnaise). Add the mustard, garlic, salt and pepper to taste, and the capers.

Using a very sharp knife, cut the fillet steak into paper thin slices – you should almost be able to see through them when held up to the light. Arrange in overlapping slices on 4 dinner plates. Garnish with lemon and serve immediately, accompanied by the sauce.

Anitra fagiano
Roast pheasant with oranges

Metric	Imperial
175 g dried chestnuts	6 oz dried chestnuts
300 ml dry white wine	½ pint dry white wine
2 medium sized pheasants, prepared	2 medium sized pheasants, prepared
salt	salt
freshly ground black pepper	freshly ground black pepper
100 g butter	4 oz butter
2 × 15 ml spoons olive oil	2 tablespoons olive oil
1 small onion, peeled and finely chopped	1 small onion, peeled and finely chopped
1 garlic clove, peeled and crushed	1 garlic clove, peeled and crushed
juice and grated rind of 1 orange	juice and grated rind of 1 orange
2 × 15 ml spoons plain flour	2 tablespoons plain flour
150 ml Marsala or sweet sherry	¼ pint Marsala or sweet sherry
200 ml Brodo di Pollo (page 8)	⅓ pint Brodo di Pollo (page 8)
3 thin-skinned oranges, peeled and segmented	3 thin-skinned oranges, peeled and segmented

Preparation time: 20–25 minutes, plus standing overnight
Cooking time: 1¼ hours
Oven: 190°C, 375°F, Gas Mark 5

Put the chestnuts into a bowl with the white wine and leave to stand overnight. Season the pheasant inside and out with salt and pepper. Heat the butter and oil in a large shallow pan and fry the onion gently for 3 minutes. Add the pheasant and lightly brown on all sides, then put into a roasting tin. Stir the garlic, orange juice and rind into the buttery juices and spoon over the pheasant. Place in a preheated oven and roast for 1 hour until just tender.
Meanwhile, put the chestnuts and their liquid into a pan and simmer for 20 minutes until tender and all the wine is absorbed.
Once the pheasant is cooked, remove it to a heated serving dish and keep warm. Tip off all but 4 × 15 ml spoons/4 tablespoons of the pheasant juices from the roasting tin. Stir the flour into the juices in the tin and cook over a gentle heat for 1 minute. Gradually stir in the Marsala and Brodo di Pollo. Bring to the boil and simmer for 2 minutes. Add the cooked chestnuts and orange segments, and heat through. Spoon some of the sauce over the pheasant and serve the remainder separately.
Serves 6

Fricassea di pollo
Chicken in egg and lemon sauce

Metric	Imperial
4 chicken joints, skinned	4 chicken joints, skinned
grated rind of 1 lemon	grated rind of 1 lemon
1 onion, peeled and thinly sliced	1 onion, peeled and thinly sliced
1 bay leaf	1 bay leaf
600 ml Brodo di Pollo (page 8)	1 pint Brodo di Pollo (page 8)
few parsley stalks	few parsley stalks
salt	salt
freshly ground white pepper	freshly ground white pepper
Sauce:	**Sauce:**
30 g butter	1 oz butter
30 g plain flour	1 oz plain flour
300 ml milk	½ pint milk
salt	salt
freshly ground white pepper	freshly ground white pepper
2 egg yolks, lightly beaten	2 egg yolks, lightly beaten
2 × 15 ml spoons chopped fresh parsley	2 tablespoons chopped fresh parsley
2 × 15 ml spoons lemon juice	2 tablespoons lemon juice

Preparation time: 10 minutes
Cooking time: 50–55 minutes

The sauce for this recipe should be very pale in colour, that is why the chicken is not fried prior to cooking, and white pepper is used in place of black pepper. As a metric equivalent to 1 oz for the butter and flour 30 g is used, to ensure a correct consistency for the sauce.

Put the chicken joints into a large shallow pan with the lemon rind, onion, bay leaf, Brodo di Pollo, parsley stalks, and salt and pepper to taste. Bring to the boil, cover and simmer for 45 minutes or until the chicken is tender. Remove the chicken joints to a heated serving dish and keep warm.
To make the sauce, strain the chicken cooking liquid. Melt the butter in a pan and stir in the flour. Cook for 1 minute, without allowing it to colour. Gradually stir in the milk and 300 ml/½ pint of the cooking liquid. Bring to the boil and simmer gently until thickened, stirring. Add salt and pepper to taste, the egg yolks, parsley and lemon juice. Heat through gently without allowing the sauce to boil. Pour the sauce over the chicken portions and serve with plain boiled noodles.

Anitra fagiano; Fricassea di pollo

VEGETABLES

The Italians have been avid producers and devourers of vegetables for many thousands of years. The Romans developed the lettuce as we now know it (at one time it did not have a head!), they introduced new varieties of cabbage, and they produced the best asparagus in the world – in fact Italy still grows the best asparagus. The people in the south of the country are great market gardeners, on a small scale that is, mainly for reasons of economy – they eke out the more expensive foods with home grown vegetables.

Peperonata
Peppers in fresh tomato sauce

Metric	Imperial
3 × 15 ml spoons olive oil	3 tablespoons olive oil
25 g butter	1 oz butter
1 large onion, peeled and thinly sliced	1 large onion, peeled and thinly sliced
1 garlic clove, peeled and crushed	1 garlic clove, peeled and crushed
4 red peppers, cored, seeded and cut into thin strips	4 red peppers, cored, seeded and cut into thin strips
8 large tomatoes, skinned and roughly chopped	8 large tomatoes, skinned and roughly chopped
salt	salt
freshly ground black pepper	freshly ground black pepper

Preparation time: 15 minutes
Cooking time: 50 minutes

Peperonata is equally good eaten hot or cold. It keeps well in the refrigerator for 2–3 days, and it is worth making a larger amount than you need. Put the prepared Peperonata into a shallow dish, and then float a thin layer of olive oil over the surface. Cover with cling film or foil and keep chilled.

Heat the oil and butter in a large pan and gently fry the onion until lightly golden. Add the garlic and pepper strips, cover and simmer for 15 minutes. Add the tomatoes and salt and pepper to taste, and cook gently for a further 30 minutes. The cooked Peperonata should be quite 'dry', but take care that it does not stick to the pan. Serve either hot or cold as a vegetable, or as part of an antipasto.

Peperonata; Fagiolini in agrodolce; Carciofi al tegame

Fagiolini in agrodolce
Green beans in sweet sour sauce

Metric	Imperial
450 g green beans, topped and tailed	1 lb green beans, topped and tailed
salt	salt
3 × 15 ml spoons granulated sugar	3 tablespoons granulated sugar
2 × 15 ml spoons water	2 tablespoons water
3 × 15 ml spoons white wine vinegar	3 tablespoons white wine vinegar
2 × 15 ml spoons chopped fresh mint	2 tablespoons chopped fresh mint
2 × 15 ml spoons sultanas	2 tablespoons sultanas
pinch of ground cloves	pinch of ground cloves
1 × 15 ml spoon pine kernels (optional)	1 tablespoon pine kernels (optional)
freshly ground black pepper	freshly ground black pepper

Preparation time: 10 minutes
Cooking time: 20 minutes

The most suitable types of beans to use for this recipe are either the small French 'haricots vert' or fat 'bobby' beans. If you find pine kernels difficult to buy, you can use shredded blanched almonds.

Leave French beans whole; cut 'bobby' beans into 5 cm/2 inch lengths. Cook the beans in boiling salted water for about 20 minutes until tender.
Meanwhile for the sauce, put the sugar and water into a saucepan and stir over a gentle heat until the sugar has dissolved. Cook briskly until the syrup turns golden. Remove the pan from the heat and stir in the remaining ingredients. Heat the sauce through. Drain the cooked beans thoroughly and toss in the sauce. Serve hot.

Carciofi al tegame
Stuffed artichokes

Metric	Imperial
4 globe artichokes, stalks removed	4 globe artichokes, stalks removed
juice of 1 lemon	juice of 1 lemon
6 × 15 ml spoons olive oil	6 tablespoons olive oil
4 × 15 ml spoons fresh breadcrumbs	4 tablespoons fresh breadcrumbs
2 × 15 ml spoons chopped fresh mint	2 tablespoons chopped fresh mint
2 garlic cloves, peeled and crushed	2 garlic cloves, peeled and crushed
2 × 15 ml spoons chopped fresh parsley	2 tablespoons chopped fresh parsley
salt	salt
freshly ground black pepper	freshly ground black pepper
150 ml white wine	1/4 pint white wine

Preparation time: 25 minutes
Cooking time: 40–45 minutes

Cut the tip off each artichoke leaf with scissors, and use a small spoon to remove the centre hairy 'choke'. Plunge the artichokes into a bowl of cold water, with the lemon juice added.
Heat 2 × 15 ml spoons/2 tablespoons of the oil in a pan and fry the breadcrumbs until golden brown. Mix the breadcrumbs with half the mint, the garlic, parsley, and salt and pepper to taste.
Drain the artichokes and pat them dry. Ease open the leaves. Press the seasoned breadcrumb mixture between the leaves. Put the artichokes upright in a saucepan. Add the remaining oil and mint, salt and pepper to taste, and the white wine. Cover and cook for 35–40 minutes until tender. Serve hot.

Crauti alla modenese; Asparagi alla toscani; Insalata di cavalfiore; Torta di patate

Crauti alla modenese
Spiced cabbage

Metric	Imperial
3 × 15 ml spoons olive oil	3 tablespoons olive oil
1 × 2.5 ml spoon ground cinnamon	½ teaspoon ground cinnamon
1 × 2.5 ml spoon ground ginger	½ teaspoon ground ginger
1 medium white cabbage, finely shredded	1 medium white cabbage, finely shredded
coarsely grated rind of 1 orange	coarsely grated rind of 1 orange
1 × 5 ml spoon brown sugar	1 teaspoon brown sugar
300 ml white wine	½ pint white wine
salt	salt
freshly ground black pepper	freshly ground black pepper

Preparation time: 5 minutes
Cooking time: 35 minutes

For a rather more unusual flavour you can add strips of candied orange peel in place of the grated orange rind and brown sugar.

Heat the oil in a large pan. Add the cinnamon and ginger and stir over the heat for 30 seconds. Add the shredded cabbage, orange rind and sugar and cook, stirring, for 3 minutes. Add the white wine and salt and pepper to taste. Cover the pan and cook gently for 30 minutes until the cabbage is just tender. Serve hot.

Asparagi alla toscani
Asparagus with anchovy sauce

Metric	Imperial
750 g asparagus	1½ lb asparagus
salt	salt
juice of 2 lemons	juice of 2 lemons
3 hard-boiled egg yolks	3 hard-boiled egg yolks
4 anchovy fillets, finely chopped	4 anchovy fillets, finely chopped
2 egg yolks	2 egg yolks
300 ml olive oil	½ pint olive oil
1 garlic clove, peeled and crushed	1 garlic clove, peeled and crushed
1 × 15 ml spoon chopped fresh parsley	1 tablespoon chopped fresh parsley
freshly ground black pepper	freshly ground black pepper

Preparation time: 20 minutes
Cooking time: 20 minutes

Trim off the tough asparagus ends and tie into 1 or 2 bundles. Cook upright in boiling water, with the juice of 1 of the lemons added, for about 20 minutes until tender, covered.
Meanwhile for the sauce, sieve the hard-boiled egg yolks into a bowl. Stir in the anchovy fillets and raw egg yolks. Whisk in the olive oil in a fine trickle, as if making mayonnaise. Add the garlic, parsley, salt and pepper to taste, and a little lemon juice. Drain the cooked asparagus and serve warm accompanied by the anchovy and egg sauce.

Insalata di cavalfiore
Hot cauliflower salad

Metric	Imperial
1 medium cauliflower, trimmed and divided into florets	1 medium cauliflower, trimmed and divided into florets
600 ml Brodo di Pollo (page 8)	1 pint Brodo di Pollo (page 8)
1 bay leaf	1 bay leaf
strip of lemon peel	strip of lemon peel
salt	salt
freshly ground black pepper	freshly ground black pepper
150 ml olive oil	1/4 pint olive oil
2 × 15 ml spoons wine vinegar	2 tablespoons wine vinegar
1 garlic clove, peeled and crushed	1 garlic clove, peeled and crushed
1 × 5 ml spoon prepared mustard	1 teaspoon prepared mustard
2 × 15 ml spoons chopped fresh parsley	2 tablespoons chopped fresh parsley

Preparation time: 20 minutes
Cooking time: 10–12 minutes

Place the cauliflower florets in a pan with the Brodo di Pollo, bay leaf, lemon peel, and salt and pepper to taste. Bring to the boil, cover and simmer for 8–10 minutes – the cauliflower should still be slightly crisp. Meanwhile, mix the remaining ingredients together, adding salt and pepper to taste. Drain the cooked cauliflower and return to the pan with the dressing. Stir over a moderate heat for 1 minute and serve.

Torta di patate
Potato and cheese pie

Metric	Imperial
4 large potatoes	4 large potatoes
4 × 15 ml spoons olive oil	4 tablespoons olive oil
175 g Mozzarella or Fontina cheese, thinly sliced	6 oz Mozzarella or Fontina cheese, thinly sliced
salt	salt
freshly ground black pepper	freshly ground black pepper
6 tomatoes, skinned, seeded and chopped	6 tomatoes, skinned, seeded and chopped
1 garlic clove, peeled and crushed	1 garlic clove, peeled and crushed
1 × 15 ml spoon chopped fresh oregano or basil	1 tablespoon chopped fresh oregano or basil

Preparation time: 20 minutes, plus cooling
Cooking time: 40 minutes
Oven: 190°C, 375°F, Gas Mark 5

Cook the potatoes in their skins in boiling water for 10 minutes. Drain and allow to cool slightly. Peel and cut the potatoes into 5 mm/1/4 inch thick slices.
Grease a shallow ovenproof dish with 1 × 15 ml spoons/1 tablespoon of the oil. Arrange alternate layers of potato and cheese in the dish, seasoning each layer with salt and pepper. Heat 2 × 15 ml spoons/2 tablespoons of the oil in a pan and add the tomato, garlic, oregano or basil, and salt and pepper to taste. Cook for 5 minutes. Spoon over the top of the potato and cheese, and sprinkle with the remaining oil. Place in a preheated oven and cook for 25 minutes.

Spinaci alla romana
Spinach with garlic

Metric	Imperial
750 g young spinach, washed	1½ lb young spinach, washed
6 × 15 ml spoons olive oil	6 tablespoons olive oil
1 garlic clove, peeled and crushed	1 garlic clove, peeled and crushed
2 × 15 ml spoons pine kernels	2 tablespoons pine kernels
2 × 15 ml spoons raisins	2 tablespoons raisins
salt	salt
freshly ground black pepper	freshly ground black pepper

Preparation time: 5 minutes
Cooking time: 5 minutes

It is important to use really young spinach leaves for this recipe as it is only cooked for a few minutes. Shredded blanched almonds can be used in place of pine kernels.

Shake the spinach dry to remove as much moisture as possible. Gently heat the olive oil in a large pan and add the garlic, pine kernels, raisins, and salt and pepper to taste. Cook, stirring, for 1 minute. Add the prepared spinach and stir over the heat for 2–3 minutes until it is hot and just starting to soften. Serve immediately.

Finocchi in besciamella
Baked fennel with cheese sauce

Metric	Imperial
4 small heads fennel	4 small heads fennel
salt	salt
juice of ½ lemon	juice of ½ lemon
300 ml Besciamella (page 45)	½ pint Besciamella (page 45)
50 g Parma ham, chopped	2 oz Parma ham, chopped
freshly ground black pepper	freshly ground black pepper
3 × 15 ml spoons grated Parmesan cheese	3 tablespoons grated Parmesan cheese

Preparation time: 15–20 minutes
Cooking time: 30–35 minutes
Oven: 190°C, 375°F, Gas Mark 5

If you find Parma ham difficult to buy, any well-flavoured British ham can be used in its place.

Trim off the feathery pieces from the top of each head of fennel and keep to one side for garnish. Remove any brown patches from the fennel with a potato peeler. Drop the fennel into a pan of boiling water, with 1 × 5 ml spoon/1 teaspoon salt and the lemon juice added. Cook the fennel for 15 minutes until just tender – test with the tip of a sharp knife. Drain the fennel and put into a shallow ovenproof dish.
Heat the Besciamella sauce through and add the ham, salt and pepper to taste, and 2 × 15 ml spoons/2 tablespoons of the Parmesan cheese. Spoon the sauce evenly over the fennel and sprinkle with the remaining cheese. Place in a preheated oven and cook for 10–15 minutes until lightly golden. Garnish with the feathery fennel tops and serve hot.

Spinaci alla romana; Finocchi in besciamella;
Barbabietole con ragù; Fagioli con le cotiche

Barbabietole con ragù
Baked beetroot with meat sauce

Metric	Imperial
3 × 15 ml spoons olive oil	3 tablespoons olive oil
1 onion, peeled and finely chopped	1 onion, peeled and finely chopped
2 sticks celery, finely chopped	2 sticks celery, finely chopped
1 large carrot, grated	1 large carrot, grated
1 garlic clove, peeled and crushed	1 garlic clove, peeled and crushed
225 g minced veal or pork	8 oz minced veal or pork
300 ml Brodo di Manzo (page 9)	½ pint Brodo di Manzo (page 9)
salt	salt
freshly ground black pepper	freshly ground black pepper
2 × 15 ml spoons chopped fresh parsley	2 tablespoons chopped fresh parsley
8 cooked beetroot, skinned and sliced	8 cooked beetroot, skinned and sliced
50 g butter, melted	2 oz butter, melted
50 g grated Parmesan cheese	2 oz grated Parmesan cheese

Preparation time: 15 minutes
Cooking time: 1 hour
Oven: 190°C, 375°F, Gas Mark 5

Heat the oil and gently fry the onion, celery and carrot for 5 minutes. Add the garlic and minced veal or pork and fry until the meat is evenly browned. Stir in the Brodo di Manzo, add salt and pepper to taste and the parsley. Cover and simmer for 30 minutes.

Arrange the beetroot slices and meat sauce in alternate layers in a greased ovenproof dish, finishing with a generous layer of sauce. Dribble over the melted butter and sprinkle with grated Parmesan cheese. Place in a preheated oven and cook for 20 minutes. Serve immediately.

Fagioli con le cotiche
Bean and sausage stew

Metric	Imperial
350 g cannellini or dried white haricot beans, soaked overnight and drained	12 oz cannellini or dried white haricot beans, soaked overnight and drained
sprig of fresh marjoram	sprig of fresh marjoram
2 bay leaves	2 bay leaves
few parsley stalks	few parsley stalks
1 onion, peeled and sliced	1 onion, peeled and sliced
Brodo di Pollo (page 8)	Brodo di Pollo (page 8)
2 × 15 ml spoons olive oil	2 tablespoons olive oil
75 g pork fat, diced	3 oz pork fat, diced
2 garlic cloves, peeled and crushed	2 garlic cloves, peeled and crushed
2 × 15 ml spoons tomato purée	2 tablespoons tomato purée
6 tomatoes, skinned, seeded and chopped	6 tomatoes, skinned, seeded and chopped
175 g Italian boiling sausage, cut into rings	6 oz Italian boiling sausage, cut into rings
salt	salt
freshly ground black pepper	freshly ground black pepper

Preparation time: 10 minutes, plus soaking
Cooking time: 2 hours

Place the drained beans in a large saucepan. Add the sprig of marjoram, bay leaves, parsley stalks, onion, and sufficient Brodo di Pollo to completely cover the beans. Bring to the boil, cover and simmer gently for 1½ hours.

Heat the olive oil in a large saucepan and fry the diced pork fat over a high heat until the fat crispens and turns golden. Add the garlic, tomato purée, chopped tomato, 200 ml/⅓ pint Brodo di Pollo, the rings of sausage, and salt and pepper to taste. Bring to the boil and add the well drained beans. Cover and simmer gently for 20 minutes. Serve piping hot.
Serves 4–6

DESSERTS

Every Italian loves a cream cake; the larger and richer the better! And yet few Italians make rich puddings and cakes at home; they reserve their indulgence for when they are eating out in restaurants and bars, or on occasions when they are tempted by one of the many street vendors. Their biscuits are wonderful – some fine and brittle, some crisp and sugary, and others flavoured with nuts or liqueur.

Granita di aranci
Orange water ice

Metric
115 g granulated sugar
600 ml water
juice of 4 large oranges,
    strained
grated rind of 1 large
    orange

Imperial
4 oz granulated sugar
1 pint water
juice of 4 large oranges,
    strained
grated rind of 1 large
    orange

To decorate:
2 oranges, divided into
    segments
4 × 15 ml spoons Marsala

To decorate:
2 oranges, divided into
    segments
4 tablespoons Marsala

Preparation time: 15 minutes, plus cooling and freezing
Cooking time: 6 minutes

Unlike a sorbet, the Italian Granita does not include whisked egg white – it is literally a frozen, sweetened fresh fruit juice. The metric measure for the sugar quantity differs from others used in the book, but this is necessary to ensure the correct density of syrup.

Put the sugar and water into a saucepan and stir over a gentle heat until the sugar has dissolved. Bring to the boil, then simmer for exactly 5 minutes. Remove the syrup from the heat and allow to cool. Stir in the strained orange juice and grated orange rind.
Pour the orange syrup into a shallow container and freeze, without stirring, until the water ice has a granular texture. Serve in tall stemmed glasses, decorated with the orange segments and sprinkled with a little Marsala.
Serves 4–6

Variations:
Granita di Limone: make the water ice, using the strained juice of 6 lemons and grated rind of 1 lemon, in place of the orange juice and rind. Decorate with a little fresh borage or mint.
For a cooling summer drink, put a generous scoop of the Granita di Aranci into a tumbler and top up with a chilled dry white Italian wine.

Gelato di pistacchio
Pistachio ice cream

Metric
8 egg yolks
600 ml single cream
100 g caster sugar
green food colouring
75 g shelled pistachios (or
    lightly toasted almonds),
    chopped

Imperial
8 egg yolks
1 pint single cream
4 oz caster sugar
green food colouring
3 oz shelled pistachios (or
    lightly toasted almonds),
    chopped

To decorate:
few extra nuts
mimosa balls (yellow or
    green)

To decorate:
few extra nuts
mimosa balls (yellow or
    green)

Preparation time: 20 minutes, plus cooling and freezing
Cooking time: 25–30 minutes

Beat the egg yolks lightly with the cream and sugar. Put the cream mixture into the top of a double saucepan or into a heatproof bowl over a pan of water. Stir over a gentle heat until the custard will coat the back of a wooden spoon. Remove from the heat and continue stirring the custard for 1–2 minutes. If the custard is 'streaky' at this stage, strain it. Add a few drops of food colouring to tint the custard pale green. Allow to cool.
Put the custard into a shallow container, cover with foil and freeze for 1 hour (or until ice crystals form around the edge of the container). Tip the semi-frozen custard into a bowl and stir thoroughly, adding the chopped nuts.
Return the custard to the container and freeze for a further 2–3 hours. The ice cream should be 'stiff' when served, but not completely solid. Scoop the ice cream into small chilled dishes and decorate with nuts and mimosa balls.
Serves 4–6

Variation:
Gelato di Caffe: add 100 g/4 oz freshly ground coffee beans to the egg yolks and cream, before cooking the custard. Leave the coffee custard to stand for at least 1 hour to infuse before straining, to draw out the maximum flavour. Freeze as above, omitting the nuts. Pour a little coffee-based liqueur over each portion of ice cream.

Granita di aranci; Gelato di pistacchio

Panforte
Candied fruit cake

Metric	Imperial
150 g clear honey	5 oz clear honey
120 g granulated sugar	4 oz granulated sugar
75 g pine kernels, chopped	3 oz pine kernels, chopped
75 g walnuts, chopped	3 oz walnuts, chopped
75 g blanched almonds, chopped	3 oz blanched almonds, chopped
75 g glacé pineapple, chopped	3 oz glacé pineapple, chopped
75 g crystallized ginger, chopped	3 oz crystallized ginger, chopped
75 g angelica, chopped	3 oz angelica, chopped
75 g pressed dates or figs, chopped	3 oz pressed dates or figs, chopped
60 g cocoa powder	2 oz cocoa powder
1 × 2.5 ml spoon ground mace	½ teaspoon ground mace
1 × 2.5 ml spoon ground coriander	½ teaspoon ground coriander
1 × 2.5 ml spoon mixed spice	½ teaspoon mixed spice
icing sugar	icing sugar

Preparation time: 8 minutes
Cooking time: about 4 minutes
Oven: 150°C, 300°F, Gas Mark 2

This speciality sweetmeat from Siena is very rich and usually served in quite small pieces, with small cups of dark espresso coffee.
You will notice that the metric measures for some of the ingredients in this recipe differ from those generally used throughout the rest of the book. Whichever column of ingredients you decide to use when making Panforte, do keep very closely to the quantities that are given.

Put the honey and sugar into a pan and stir over a gentle heat until dissolved. Bring to the boil and boil gently until the mixture reaches 'soft ball' stage (114°C/238°F) – a little of the mixture should form a soft ball when dropped into a cup of cold water. Remove the pan from the heat and stir the pine kernels, walnuts, almonds, pineapple, ginger, angelica, dates or figs, cocoa, mace, coriander and mixed spice into the honey syrup. It will be quite stiff at this stage of preparation.
Press the mixture into a greased 20–23 cm/8–9 inch loose-bottomed flan tin (preferably one with fluted sides). Place in a preheated oven and bake for 30 minutes. Lift the Panforte out on its tin base and allow to cool on a wire tray. Dredge with sifted icing sugar and serve cut into thin wedges. Store in an airtight tin.
Makes about 18–20 thin wedges

Torta di noci e canditi
Walnut and candied peel pie

Metric	Imperial
450 g puff pastry	1 lb puff pastry
175 g Mascherpone cheese or any full fat soft cheese	6 oz Mascherpone cheese or any full fat soft cheese
50 g caster sugar	2 oz caster sugar
2 × 15 ml spoons apricot jam	2 tablespoons apricot jam
3 egg yolks	3 egg yolks
50 g walnuts, chopped	2 oz walnuts, chopped
100 g chopped candied mixed peel	4 oz chopped candied mixed peel
finely grated rind of 1 lemon	finely grated rind of 1 lemon

To decorate:	**To decorate:**
2 × 15 ml spoons coarsely chopped walnuts	2 tablespoons coarsely chopped walnuts
icing sugar	icing sugar

Preparation time: 20 minutes
Cooking time: 35–40 minutes
Oven: 200°C, 400°F, Gas Mark 6

Mascherpone is a soft, creamy, bland Italian cheese and the flavour closely resembles that of clotted cream. If you find it difficult to buy, use a good quality full fat soft cheese – most supermarkets and good food stores sell it either loose or pre-packed.

Roll out the puff pastry fairly thinly. Line a 23 cm/9 inch fluted flan tin with half the pastry. Beat the soft cheese with the sugar, apricot jam, 2 of the egg yolks, the chopped walnuts, peel and lemon rind. Spoon into the pastry case. Cover the filling with the remaining pastry, trimming off any overlapping pastry. Pinch the pastry edges together to seal.
Beat the remaining egg yolk with a little water and brush over the top of the pie to glaze. Place in a preheated oven and bake for 35–40 minutes until risen and deep golden brown. Sprinkle with the walnuts and dust with sifted icing sugar. Serve either straight from the oven, or cold.
Serves 6–8

Torta di noci e canditi; Panforte

Biscotti all'arancio
Spiced orange biscuits

Metric	*Imperial*
225 g plain flour	8 oz plain flour
generous pinch of ground cinnamon	generous pinch of ground cinnamon
generous pinch of mixed spice	generous pinch of mixed spice
75 g caster sugar	3 oz caster sugar
150 g butter, softened	5 oz butter, softened
2 egg yolks	2 egg yolks
finely grated rind of 1 orange	finely grated rind of 1 orange
1 × 2.5 ml spoon ground aniseed	½ teaspoon ground aniseed
75 g plain chocolate, melted, to decorate	3 oz plain chocolate, melted, to decorate

Preparation time: 25 minutes, plus chilling
Cooking time: 10–12 minutes
Oven: 190°C, 375°F, Gas Mark 5

Sift the flour, cinnamon and mixed spice into a bowl. Add the caster sugar, butter, egg yolks, orange rind and aniseed, and work to a smooth dough – you will find this easier to do by hand, rather than with a spoon. Wrap in foil or cling film and chill for 1 hour. Using a large piping bag fitted with a large star nozzle, pipe 10 cm/4 inch lengths on lightly greased baking sheets. Place in a preheated oven and bake 10–12 minutes until lightly golden. Remove the biscuits to a wire tray and allow to cool.
Dip one end of each biscuit into the melted chocolate. Place on a sheet of greased greaseproof paper until the chocolate has set.

Biscotti all'arancio; Zabaione caldo; Pesche allo zabaione

Zabaione caldo
Hot marsala dessert

Metric	Imperial
6 egg yolks	6 egg yolks
4 × 15 ml spoons caster sugar	4 tablespoons caster sugar
250 ml Marsala	8 fl oz Marsala
grated nutmeg, to finish	grated nutmeg, to finish

Preparation time: 3 minutes
Cooking time: 5–8 minutes

Zabaione (sometimes zabaglione) is one of the classic Italian puddings. It should be made with Marsala, but if this is not available, a medium sweet sherry can be used instead.

Put the egg yolks and caster sugar into the top of a double saucepan or into a heatproof bowl. Whisk until thick, light and creamy, and then gradually whisk in the Marsala. Stand the mixture over a pan of gently simmering water, and continue whisking until the Zabaione is very thick and will leave a trail – lift the whisk free from the mixture, and any Zabaione that falls back should lay in a 'ribbon' on the surface.
As soon as the Zabaione has reached this stage, remove from the heat and spoon into warmed stemmed glasses, allowing a small amount to form a teardrop over the rim of each glass. Sprinkle with grated nutmeg and serve immediately.
Serves 4–6

Pesche allo zabaione
Peaches with marsala sauce

Metric	Imperial
4 large ripe peaches, skinned	4 large ripe peaches, skinned
150 ml Marsala or medium sweet sherry	¼ pint Marsala or medium sweet sherry
3 eggs yolks	3 egg yolks
75 g caster sugar	3 oz caster sugar
finely grated rind of ½ lemon	finely grated rind of ½ lemon
150 ml double or whipping cream, whipped	¼ pint double or whipping cream, whipped

To decorate:	To decorate:
50 g chopped candied mixed peel	2 oz chopped candied mixed peel
25 g shelled pistachios, chopped	1 oz shelled pistachios, chopped

Preparation time: 35 minutes, plus chilling
Cooking time: 8–10 minutes

Put the skinned peaches into a shallow dish and prick at regular intervals with a fine skewer. Spoon over half the Marsala. Cover the peaches and chill for 1 hour. Drain off the Marsala from the peaches and reserve. Put the egg yolks, caster sugar and lemon rind into a heatproof bowl, and whisk until thick, light and creamy. Gradually whisk in the Marsala and the reserved Marsala drained from the peaches. Stand the bowl over a pan of gently simmering water and stir the Marsala sauce continuously until thick enough to coat the back of a spoon. Remove the bowl from the heat and whisk the sauce until it cools. Fold the whipped cream into the Marsala sauce.
Spoon the sauce over the peaches and chill for a further 2 hours. Sprinkle with the peel and pistachios before serving.

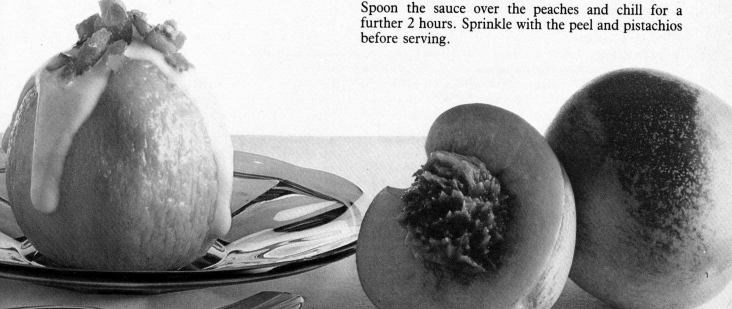

Sfogliatelle
Fan-shaped pastries

Metric	Imperial
350 g puff pastry	12 oz puff pastry
2 × 5 ml spoons caster sugar	2 teaspoons caster sugar
1 egg white, lightly whisked	1 egg white, lightly whisked
icing sugar	icing sugar

Filling:

100 g Ricotta cheese	4 oz Ricotta cheese
2 × 15 ml spoons caster sugar	2 tablespoons caster sugar
150 ml double or whipping cream, whipped	1/4 pint double or whipping cream, whipped
4 × 15 ml spoons chopped candied or glacé fruits	4 tablespoons chopped candied or glacé fruits

Preparation time: 35 minutes, plus chilling and cooling
Cooking time: 10–12 minutes
Oven: 200°C, 400°F, Gas Mark 6

The filling for these little pastries can be flavoured with a spoonful or two of liqueur if liked – Galliano or Aurum would be the best choice.

Roll out the pastry thinly. Using a tea-plate as a guide, cut out 4 circles each 18 cm/7 inches in diameter. Cut each pastry circle in half, and then in half again, to give 16 equal sections of pastry. Trim the rounded side of each pastry section with a pastry wheel or pinking shears. Place on lightly greased baking sheets and chill for 30 minutes.
Stir the sugar into the egg white. Brush the glaze over each section of pastry. Place in a preheated oven and bake for 10–12 minutes until risen, puffed and lightly golden. Remove the pastries to a wire tray and make a split along the crinkled side of each pastry. Allow them to go cold.
For the filling, soften the Ricotta in a bowl. Add the caster sugar to the whipped cream and blend with the cheese. Stir in the chopped fruits. Make a 'pocket' in each pastry where it is split, and fill with the cheese and fruit mixture. Dust with sifted icing sugar.
Makes 16 small pastries

Castagne alla crema
Chestnut and strega pudding

Metric	Imperial
1 × 425 g can unsweetened chestnut purée	1 × 15 oz can unsweetened chestnut purée
4 × 15 ml spoons caster sugar	4 tablespoons caster sugar
100 g plain chocolate, melted	4 oz plain chocolate, melted
3 × 15 ml spoons Strega liqueur	3 tablespoons Strega liqueur
300 ml double or whipping cream, thickly whipped	1/2 pint double or whipping cream, thickly whipped

To decorate:

300 ml double or whipping cream	1/2 pint double or whipping cream
2 × 15 ml spoons Strega liqueur	2 tablespoons Strega liqueur
chopped pine nuts (optional)	chopped pine nuts (optional)

Preparation time: 25 minutes, plus chilling

This delicious chestnut pudding can be frozen and served like an ice cream. Freeze the mixture in a shallow container, and remove from the freezer 10–15 minutes before serving. Scoop the frozen chestnut mixture into small glass dishes and pour a little Strega liqueur over each portion.

Beat the chestnut purée with the sugar, melted chocolate and Strega until smooth. Fold the whipped cream into the chestnut mixture. Chill for 2 hours.
Using a piping bag fitted with a plain wide nozzle, pipe the chestnut mixture into a conical shape on a serving dish. Chill for a further 2 hours. To decorate the pudding, whip the cream with the Strega until quite thick. Swirl the cream around the sides of the pudding. Decorate with the chopped pine nuts.
Serves 6

From the left: Sfogliatelle;
Budino al cioccolato; Castagne alla crema

Budino al cioccolato
Chocolate pudding

Metric
4 egg yolks
75 g caster sugar
225 g Ricotta cheese
1 × 15 ml spoon instant
  coffee powder
2 × 15 ml spoons boiling
  water
175 g plain chocolate,
  melted
300 ml double or whipping
  cream, whipped

To decorate:
50 g plain chocolate,
  coarsely grated
coffee beans

Imperial
4 egg yolks
3 oz caster sugar
8 oz Ricotta cheese
1 tablespoon instant coffee
  powder
2 tablespoons boiling
  water
6 oz plain chocolate,
  melted
1/2 pint double or whipping
  cream, whipped

To decorate:
2 oz plain chocolate,
  coarsely grated
coffee beans

Preparation time: 25 minutes, plus chilling

If you find difficulty in buying Ricotta cheese, you can use sieved cottage cheese in its place.

Put the egg yolks and caster sugar into a bowl and whisk until thick, light and creamy. Beat in the Ricotta cheese, instant coffee dissolved in the boiling water, and the melted chocolate. Fold the whipped cream lightly but thoroughly into the chocolate mixture. Either spoon the mixture into 6 tall stemmed glasses, or into a large decorative glass bowl. Chill for 3–4 hours before serving. Decorate with the grated chocolate and coffee beans.
Serves 6–8

INDEX